Praise

"Excellent. This book offers a deep, wide range of insights to help both Enneagram students and newcomers discover the depth of the system and its many meaningful applications.

By letting individuals speak through and about their personality styles, the book reveals their struggles and solutions. Plus, it guides readers down their own road to growing and changing and living a more complete life."

— **Tom Condon,** Enneagram teacher and author

"Readers looking for insights on their own very human journey will find in this book a valuable resource for further examining their lives. Through the voices of individuals who have found the Enneagram to be an important part of their transformational journey, Mary Bast and CJ Fitzsimons illuminate the intriguing and paradoxical dynamic of experiencing oneself as "somebody" and "nobody.""

— **Roxanne Howe-Murphy, Ed.D,** Author, *Deep Coaching: Using the Enneagram As a Catalyst for Profound Change,* and *Deep Living: Transforming Your Relationship to Everything That Matters through the Enneagram*

"There are now many books available on the Enneagram, describing different elements of the nine personality types or styles. Some of these books use first hand reports from people of the nine different Enneagram types to help explain what the experience of that type is like. But just describing the types, while valuable, will only take us so far when we are actually interested in genuine psychological and spiritual development. in *Somebody? Nobody? The Enneagram, Mindfulness, and Life's Unfolding*, CJ and Mary have done something unique and important by focusing on each type's first-hand reports of what brought real development. The stories they present are highly resonant, relevant, and make clear how key elements of the transformational journey of each type unfold in specific and personal

ways. This book is a great contribution and resource for those using the Enneagram on the path of awakening."
— **Russ Hudson**, Co-author of *The Wisdom of the Enneagram*

"The Somebody / Nobody thread in this book is mirrored by the process people typically use to explore the Enneagram. When first introduced people pour over lists of characteristics of type to find out where they sit on the Enneagram. We need to be a Somebody first. It is only in workshop settings seeing and hearing examplars of type that we can really get the dynamics of each point. Mary and CJ have made this leap in book form through the rich intelligent reporting of 18 awake and aware individuals who share the stories of their journeys through the lens of the Enneagram. The Enneagram is made human and whole and we can recognize ourselves. Having a practice or being on a path is not formulaic: it is alchemical, and these wonderful stories and rich commentary shine a light on the process of transformation."
— **Sandy McMullen,** Artist / Author of "Inner Landscapes" and Coach

"Much like old friends catching up on a cozy couch, after a long time of not seeing one another, Mary and CJ hold a space for you to share the journey of self-reflection with a gentle tug. So, pull up a chair, tuck in your feet, and bring yourself to this book with the presence of mind it implores. Inside, each human exemplar speaks with a candor that lends an utterly truthful tone to the telling of "type." In turn, our authors weave their own authentic voices, through an application of the Enneagram, which leaves us knowing – without a doubt – that the struggle of being human is more than okay, it is necessary. If you are a lover of people, as I am, you will appreciate the gamut we run on the map of human experience, laid out on the pages within. And if, like me, you are also one who seeks to catch the subtle ways in which we each deftly avoid our true selves, you will find this a compelling avenue to bring you back inside yourself."
— **Susan Olesek,** Founder, Enneagram Prison Project

"Mary and CJ did a beautiful job of telling and interpreting inspirational stories of transformation. I especially like that they have mostly been lived in ordinary contexts, by people who are candidates to "be in the world without being of the world", following Gurdjieff's concept. The result is an engaging and easy-reading book that brings to surface many subtleties of the inner work, while showing why there are at least as many paths as people on Earth. Provided that they help us become both somebody and nobody."

— **Uranio Paes**, Director of UP9

"The old song and Zen parable tell us, "First there is a mountain, then there is no mountain, then there is." The personal narratives in this book—stories from the heart rather than the textbook—show people on the trip up the mountain, people wrestling with the ongoing journey of finding yourself so you can lose yourself and ultimately find yourself again. These are stories of real people speaking about themselves with authenticity, not narratives based on theory or speculation about what goes on in the minds of others. Ironically, it is the naturalness of these stories that validate the theory. There is much to learn about the Enneagram in these pages."

— **Mario Sikora**, *Co-Author of* Awareness to Action

"I applaud the approach Mary and CJ have taken. Instead of imposing abstract Enneagram theory on the person, let the person tell you from their own lived experience. I found each contributor's reflections and testaments both honest and humble – including the authors'. Thanks Mary and CJ for collecting, editing, and commenting on these essays; and thank you, participants, for writing them. You enrich our understanding and empathy for each type and give us direction and hope for transforming our own lives from somebody to nobody."

— **Jerome P. Wagner, Ph.D.**, Author of *Enneagram Spectrum of Personality Styles* and *Nine Lenses on the World: the Enneagram Perspective*

Somebody? Nobody?

The Enneagram, Mindfulness and Life's Unfolding

Mary Bast, Ph.D.

and

CJ Fitzsimons, Ph.D.

Copyright © 2017 by Mary Bast and CJ Fitzsimons

All rights reserved

Published in Germany by
Leadership Sculptor Press.
Registered Office: Laubstrasse 1
76530 Baden-Baden, Germany

ISBN 978-3-9819000-0-2

www.leadershipsculptor.com

First Edition

Cover Design: Laura Waters
Book Design: CJ Fitzsimons
Cover art: "Dark Night of the Soul" by Mary Bast, Oil on canvas
www.marybast.com

Contents

Foreword by Jerome P. Wagner, Ph.D.
i

Chapter 0
1

Chapter 1 – Style 1
5

1. Evolution of Consciousness – Alison's story	5
2. Everything Has Sanctity – Kevin's story	12
3. Commentary	17

Chapter 2 – Style 2
21

1. Breaking Down the Illusions – Jessica's story	21
2. Staying Awake – Bryan's story	30
3. Commentary	36

Chapter 3 – Style 3
39

1. The Seasons of our Lives – Grant's story	39
2. Level by Level – Valerie's story	45
3. Commentary	52

Chapter 4 – Style 4
55

1. Leaving the Drama Behind – Kathryn's story	55
2. The Richness of Being Real – Foster's Story	62
3. Commentary	70

Chapter 5 – Style 5
73

1. Out of the Biosphere – Peter's story	73
2. The Hero's Story – David's Story	77
3. Commentary	81

Chapter 6 – Style 6
85

1. Riding the Bull – Bill's story	85
2. Joy Moves It Along – Jim's Story	92
3. Commentary	97

Chapter 7 – Style 7
104

1. Mosaic – Jessica's story	101
2. Altered States – Alan's Story	112
3. Commentary	120

Chapter 8 – Style 8
123

1. Gathering Courage – Ursula's story	123
2. Out of the Box – Jeff's Story	127
3. Commentary	133

Chapter 9 – Style 9
137

1. Boxes and Spheres Moving Through Time – Claire's story	137
2. Two Steps Forward, One Step Back – Ralph's Story	144
3. Commentary	150

Chapter 10 – Afterword
153
About the Author
169
About Leadership Sculptor
171

Foreword

I appreciate the approach Mary and CJ have taken – no doubt because it's the way I went about learning the Enneagram styles. Back in the early 1970's in Chicago, Bob Ochs, S.J. taught a two-semester class called *Religious Experience*. The spine of the course was the Enneagram, which he had just learned from Claudio Naranjo in Berkeley. We received the theory from Ochs along with some wonderful examples from his and Claudio's experience. I then had the opportunity to informally interview my fellow classmates about how these Enneagram dynamics showed up in their own lives. Because the Enneagram basically "spilled the beans" about all of us, I found people wonderfully honest and forthcoming about themselves. We knew a lot about each other anyway, and the Enneagram gave us the occasion to talk about ourselves in a very open manner.

Some theorists have focused on the Enneagram map, making it more elaborate and detailed. But they haven't connected the map to the territory of people's lived experience, demonstrating that it's possible to come up with a very sophisticated map that bears little relevance to the territory itself.

Mary and CJ have gone back to the territory. They've asked style exemplars to talk about their lived experience. I found each contributor's reflections and testaments both honest and humble – including the authors'. It's similar to the experience I had 40 years ago (it seems only yesterday). The phenomenologists advise us to go back to the data itself to let our theory come out of the experience. Do *exegesis*, reading out of the text, rather than *eisegesis*, reading your theory into the data.

CJ's comments on participants' reflections derive from their writing. He's not putting words in their mouths but honoring the words coming out of their mouths.

Hearing from individuals themselves is much more satisfying and illuminating than studying pure theory. I hope I haven't endangered my membership in the "Five" club by saying this.

I believe this is why presenters teach using panels of style exemplars rather than relying on lecture alone. The lecturer can speak authoritatively about one style – their own. They are relying on hearsay when they describe the eight other styles. Better to hear from the horse's mouth than the horse's… (mouthpiece).

Transformation can be a very abstract concept. I often find descriptions of trans-personal and pre-personal experiences rather tenuous. I do better in the personal range. The "farther reaches of human nature" (Maslow's phrase) and the psychoses are hard to grasp unless you've been there. Fortunately and unfortunately we all have the potential to tap into either extreme.

Reading about people who have been there is a great help in understanding personal transformations. In contrast to infants who leave the womb but don't come back to the womb to say what it's like out there or individuals who have died who don't come back to tell us what it's like over there, we have some folks here who can tell us about their journey to a different state. We owe them our thanks for doing so.

We also owe our thanks to Oscar Ichazo for writing about the "divine ideas," the psychocatalyzers that transform our thoughts into authentic apprehensions and appraisals of reality. Once we get those "ideas" we grasp reality as it is. My understanding is that these "ideas" align us with our true nature. On a less exalted plane, I've described the "divine ideas" as adaptive cognitive schemas and the "virtues" as adaptive emotional schemas, residing in our higher self, that are more useful because they are more accurate than the distorting lenses (maladaptive cognitive schemas) and vices (maladaptive emotional schemas) of our compensating personality. See what happens when you get too abstract! You'll have a better sense of this when you read the testimonies of the people in the following chapters.

The process of transforming is like personality itself: our transformation is like everyone else's (we share a common human nature); it is like some others' transformations (we share a similar style); and it is like no one else's (we are each unique).

Going from *somebody to nobody* is a process we eventually all share whether we want to or not. I suppose you could also say we go from *somebody to everybody* when our sense of self expands to include all of reality, when we realize we are all interwoven into the fabric of life.

I do agree we need to have formed a self before we can transform or get past our self. I recall someone observing – as he reflected on the three vows of poverty, chastity, and obedience – that we shouldn't give up possessions until we've actually been able to earn possessions. We shouldn't give up sex until we've fully experienced our sexuality. And we shouldn't give up our will to another until we've developed our will and established our independence. You can't give up something you've never had.

It does seem like a waste of the first half of our lives to go to all the trouble of creating a self only to relinquish that self in the second half of our lives. Nevertheless we do need that vehicle to get us down the road of life. Then we can trade in the antiquated form of transportation. The individuals gathered here tell us it's not so scary or awful to be transformed and move on. Actually it is *awe*-ful if we take the risk, or when destiny pushes us into the unfamiliar.

Enjoy the trip. And may you be blessed with good companions like these who are along for the ride.

Jerome P. Wagner, Ph.D.   *Chicago, September 2017*

Chapter Zero - Introduction

Over the years, Mary interviewed people of all nine Enneagram styles about their everyday experience of the transformation process. In the beginning, she thought the path would be somewhat linear, even expected there might be a point of arrival. From our experience and reflections by our clients, however, we've found that observing and letting go of habitual patterns is a complex and continuing journey.

Many people have recalled a strengthening of their self-esteem as they first matured emotionally, which could be seen paradoxically as deepening their Enneagram trance. But they were clearly shifting to a new and necessary self-awareness and self-acceptance.

In *Paths Beyond Ego* John Engler wrote, "You have to be somebody before you can be nobody," suggesting we can't surrender our ego-patterns until we've developed a sense of self and can begin to see how that self operates. This strikes us as a great truth and explains what we've found in these interviews. Respondents typically grow into their personalities before they can begin to surrender. And having surrendered, these personalities mutiny again at some point. Indeed, people seem to go in and out of *somebody* and *nobody*, depending upon the particular aspect of self under scrutiny and the nature of their worldview and life experience.

An Enneagram Two said, for example, "My parents had been critical, and my husband cut me down all the time. I was miserable, even thinking about taking my life. But I realized, *Hey, I've got four children. I have to find a shrink!* Until therapy, nobody in my lifetime had ever told me I was good, sensitive, caring. That was transforming." She was clearly becoming *somebody*.

Another Two said, "My worldview has become far more expansive. I've let go of a lot of control needs. I'm in a relationship predicated on health and respect for individuality." This sounds more like becoming *nobody*, but for all we know that could have been simply a peak in his lifelong trek.

An additional complexity we've found is that Enneagram worldviews are so deeply rooted they may trick us into thinking our witness is the *nobody* essence when, actually, *somebody* is still in charge. A Nine said, for example, "For me the quest has involved figuring out where and how I begin to negate myself. To my horror, I discovered the voice I thought was a built-in Buddhist spiritual

1

director (*What's the compassionate thing to do here?*) was only another way to lose my self in being a 'good' Nine, a rationale to erase myself and merge with others' needs."

How do you know when it's your essence calling and not ego? In answer to this question an Enneagram Five said, "Trying to make this distinction is metaphysical balderdash. I trust that whatever is happening is all I have to work with, no less, no more. I don't believe it's possible to be off the path."

As you read the stories to follow, decide for yourself:
- Is it possible to be off the path?
- Does it make sense that some of our transformational experiences prepare us to have a self before we can begin transforming to no-self?
- Is the path straightforward?

In keeping with the subject matter, we have opted for a simple format. Each of the nine chapters contains two stories of how representatives of that Enneagram style are seeking and finding their own answers to the *Somebody? Nobody?* conundrum. Rounding out each chapter, CJ has added a brief commentary that underlines the major shifts in the stories from an Enneagram perspective and provides a few questions to ponder. We close by reflecting on our own journeys and how development of the book has impacted us.

For a project like this to come together many helping hands and minds are required. First and foremost we thank those who shared their inspiring stories with us, anonymously renamed Alan, Alison, Bill, Bryan, Claire, David, Foster, Grant, Jeff, Jessica, Jim, Kathryn, Kevin, Peter, Ralph, Ursula, and Valerie. Without your journey and generosity there would be no book. We also thank Mario Sikora, who has encouraged this project and our collaboration since its early days; Peter McNab, for encouraging the serialization of excerpts from the book in *Nine Points Magazine*; and Jerry Wagner for his gracious foreword.

Contents

1. Evolution of Consciousness – Alison's story   5

2. Everything Has Sanctity – Kevin's story   12

3. Commentary   17

Chapter One – Style One

Evolution of Consciousness – Alison's story

My notion of goodness or rightness has shifted over the years, so in that sense there's been some transformation. But I'm nervous about a word that to my mind sounds a bit pretentious. For me there's been an evolution of consciousness. In my earlier years I spent more time at my Four stress point, and in recent years more time in the direction of my security point, Seven. I also think there's been some movement from being more in the Nine wing to being in a much stronger Two wing. So there has been a shift within the One worldview that it's important to be impeccable. My notion of impeccability has shifted over the years, become a little deeper, a little less nit-picky in terms of, *Oh, we've got to look perfect*. We've got to have every hair in place. We have to give perfect dinner parties. Now, it's more, What is the perfect way of helping this person? Or maybe not helping, of just getting out of the way.

I'm interested in Gurdjieff's concept of shock points. There certainly have been some in my life. My divorce from my first husband was a big leap into the abyss, as in Castaneda's image of jumping off a cliff. Another shock point was dealing with a serious accident my partner had, taking care of him over a long period of recovery. Another was learning about the Enneagram, becoming aware of its implications for my own life. Prior to that I'd assumed everybody thought the way I did and was aware of right and wrong, that people couldn't be good if they didn't do what was clearly right. It never occurred to me that others might have a different focus of attention than I do. That opened up the question, *If I could be so mistaken about the way the world is, could I not be mistaken about a great many other things*?

The transition in my career, although more gradual, was also something of a shock – from earning a living as an actress to a middle-age career as an editor and a writer. It was a transition, certainly, into seeing myself quite differently, into a sense of security about having mastered certain skills, which are a little more difficult to pin down when you're an actress. There are certainly skills and techniques I learned, but my security as an editor and as a writer is a lot firmer. If I have something to say, I have a fair amount of confidence in my ability to say it with clarity and a certain amount of eloquence.

When I was in my Four period, most of my really bad sufferings had to do with romantic fixations. As a teenager, as a college student, even in my adult life until my late thirties, there were episodes of being left by or being rejected by, or not having interest from a person I was fixated on. It was obsessional, not being able to let go of hurt and really flogging my own sufferings. And a fair amount of the poetry I wrote at this time was celebrating that kind of suffering. I look back at it now and I think, *Boy, that person was really in a bad way!* I'm not there anymore, yet I remember and sympathize.

I think the One at Four is very different from the Four at Four. The One at Four is combining the obsessive-compulsive aspect with the self-pity, the self-dramatization, a habit of melancholy, mentally playing with the idea of suicide. I never seriously considered suicide, but there were a few times when I thought, *Oh, if it gets too bad I can always do that.* I never made any kind of plan, let alone an attempt, but I was wretchedly unhappy for years at a time. I think the fairly healthy One is focused very much on tasks, on meaningful work, and I'd lost my grip in terms of focus on my career. I coasted, did auditions, did jobs, but didn't have any intelligent plan or a very intelligent attitude about it. I was just fixated on all this stuff that was going round and round in my mind. It finally got worn out. It's like playing a record over and over again; eventually you wear out the grooves. Psychologists would call it an extinction procedure. You eventually extinguish the thing by going over and over it so many times, it wears itself out on some level that's psychological but feels physiological, too.

A number of factors have led to my growing up. The first was to meet my partner – far and away the most important factor in my evolution, partly because I was terribly insecure about myself, about my value, my attractiveness, all of it. We're all changed by love. And the fact that this absolutely wonderful man could not only love me but keep on loving me unconditionally had to change me. It's been a very rich relationship, and he's changed a lot, too. Not that I've had any program to change him, but I've seen a shift in him from being much more suspicious and negative about romance, to really blossoming and becoming far more creative. We've not done any program of working on the relationship. It's just having a really loving friend whom you know has your interests at heart and is truly on your side. We have wonderful conversations. He's in favor of my becoming my best self as I conceive that and I want him to be the best self he can conceive of being. And I want to help him be that.

Becoming involved with regular meditation has been a huge factor in terms of getting a picture of my own monkey mind, the way it races around and goes in 15 directions. I was beginning to have symptoms of an ulcer and I'd read well-founded scientific evidence that meditation had effects on certain physiological patterns, and I thought, *My God! I am really going in a bad direction here. I've got to find a way out of it and here's a technique. I'm going to do it!* So I took a Transcendental Meditation course and have been doing regular meditation ever since. Not that I feel I've gotten good at meditation, but it's given me moments of clarity where I can *see* myself. And it's also given me a strong sense that there's not an end to life with death – that there is a consciousness that is fixed and goes on beyond the body – because I've had a real sense of separate consciousness. As a result of my experience with meditation, the personality also seems to me a garment that we put on, like the body. I came to that belief before I ever knew the Enneagram. And the Enneagram seems to reinforce that our personality, our fixations, our preoccupations are also garments.

Body work has been another really important factor in making me aware of my own process, a fabulous way of coming to look at the anger Ones tend to deny – neo-Reichian work, bio-energetics, any exercises that involve bringing up anger; something as simple as pounding a pillow that brings up a lot of rage, and then pain and sadness. I used to think, pre-meditation, that if I ever let my anger escape, it would be this volcano that would devastate the countryside for miles around! Especially through the body work, I learned there are ways to release it and you don't devastate the countryside, no one dies, and no tragedy occurs. So you come to allow the lid to rest a little more lightly on the pot. You're not pushing it down so hard for fear the contents will explode. It's not quite such a pressure cooker. I'm more in touch with my anger than I was when I was younger. I'm aware when it comes up, I don't always squash it; I sometimes at least let it be expressed one way or another.

A vivid insight for me was the pattern created by imbalance of centers as conceived by Riso and Hudson for the One – that the moving center is inadequate, so one flogs it with feelings, using the feeling center to enhance, to hype, to add wattage to the moving center. The thinking center is off to the side uninvolved in this little drama. It made me suddenly aware of this pattern in my work life, where I'd done nothing to avoid situations in which I'd have a grievance with someone, thus have an excuse to get angry, and the anger would allow me to separate from them and go off to do creative projects on my own. I thought, *Oh, my God, this is appalling*! I'd never doubted that I have passionate feelings; but the fact that I'd used them to get myself into motion – to enhance what I perceived as inadequate will power – shocked me.

I asked myself, *Do I really need to follow this pattern? Is there some other way? Could some fuel other than anger get me in motion?* And I answered, *Yes, there's love! And I love what I'm doing. Is it not possible simply to allow that love to carry the day?*

Finding life work for myself has been a tremendous help in focusing my energies. It's so lovely to find the work you were born to do. All the disparate experiences that seemed so unconnected suddenly all fit together. My work as a writer, a teacher of English, an actress, even things I loathed doing at the time to make a living – like telemarketing – turned out to have an integral part in this combination of skills, abilities, and sensitivities I need to do the work I want to do. I'm doing it for love, and it feels very freeing.

As a child I felt extremely inept socially, feeling that nobody liked me. I read about the Social Four feeling like an outsider, and that Four-ish aspect was there. Although I did have a few good friends, I didn't have many friends, didn't really know how to play the game. As an adult it's a skill I've cultivated. I have a good network of friends and I've made a strong effort to help them meet each other and support each other. I organized a women's group that meets once a month or so. I've learned how to *be* a friend and so, not surprisingly, I *have* friends. Ones can be very much in their fixation, rigid with themselves and rigid in their expectations of others. I'm a Sexual One and one-to-one relationship is particularly important for me, but I think friendships are important for any One, where you are accepted not because you're perfect but just because you're a valuable person, and you come to accept other people not just because they're perfect but because they are whoever they are.

For me learning how to be a friend has come partly out of watching the amazing man I live with, his skills with people, his empathy, and his easy connection with people, getting a sense of his mind set, his heart set that allows him to make that connection, and seeing him make that connection with me.

These changes have not been so much an idea of "working" on myself as having been blessed with situations where there was insight about the patterns, usually through a fair amount of pain. I think of a workshop where I went through all the rejection and the insecurity, reliving all I had dealt with in my childhood and my youth. It all came back, and I was just wretched, and then there was a wonderful sense of clarity about that pattern. But it's not been *Oh, I'm going to fix X in my personality*. I don't see it as a program of work, a schedule of something I'm going to accomplish by date X. I've never worked on myself in that way. It's more, *If I can just remain aware, if I can allow the insights to come in when they're available and then act on them.*

"Impeccability" is a word that means a lot to me. I remember my mother saying, "If a thing is worth doing it's worth doing well," and that always seemed to me to be true. It drives me crazy if my partner just throws together making his bed and it's all messy. I take the time and the care to do it right. He'll wash the dishes and there will be grease all over the dishes. When I wash the dishes, they're washed. I try not to get on his case, to let him be who he is. But then I sneak in and do the bed right. I figure I need to take care of things that trouble me and not expect him to take care of them, because he doesn't value them.

That's an interesting vignette of the way things have shifted. As a child my sister and I were expected after dinner to wash the dishes. My mother had cooked dinner and it was not an unreasonable thing to expect, but I absolutely hated it and felt oppressed. I did it all right, I suppose, but I wasn't particularly conscious of taking care with it. Now I almost enjoy washing the dishes. There's a meditative quality of doing the task in an efficient way and a simple way.

I think of Feldenkrais *awareness through movement*, which is another experience that has given me insight into exactly the right amount of energy for a task. It's a great aesthetic pleasure to know when you open a door you don't need to turn the knob so hard, but to have confidence of exactly the right amount of effort.

The Feldenkrais work was important in coming to understand my physical capabilities. As a child I was given lessons in ballet and tap dancing and acrobatics because I was fairly awkward. I don't mean to suggest I was disabled, just a bit awkward. When you do this work, you become aware of effortfulness in spheres that aren't even physical. In writing, for example, it doesn't work when you try. A relationship, in some way, doesn't work when you try; it works when you clear things away and allow the goodness in both of you to be there. My partner and I have had fights, God knows, but the *trying* thing has been a real bane of my life. To stop effortfulness stops flogging the will with emotion, stops the overkill – which was only taking place because of insecurity.

A very good experience for me was Julia Cameron's *The Artist's Way*, a twelve-week program exploring your own pleasure and joy in creativity – not just in art, but an artist's view of the world. With the One's discipline and follow-through, I did all twelve weeks, all she said to do, and it was a wonderful exploration of my own joy in creativity, a melding of the Four and Seven barriers.

So all these pieces have said, *See, there is a different way to do this.* And I've allowed myself to experience the different ways and see they are indeed more impeccable. At the end of a workshop I once attended, we talked about a mantra for the One to improve the possibility of illumination or growth. There's a sense in Ones that if we don't work really hard at it, it won't be enough; trusting the *enoughness* of our own gifts and respecting them is very difficult. So I came up with, "Let it be." Just *let it be, let the process work through you, don't try to work it but let its possibilities inhabit you.*

I was in a point group in a Palmer workshop on defense mechanisms, and we talked about exercises we might devise for Ones to help us become aware when we're in our fixation. I devised one that if someone asks a question and you know the answer, to not say anything, to sit with your own rightness without needing to advertise it. At the end of one of Naranjo's workshops he asked us what exercise we could set for ourselves that would be in the direction of virtue, in the One's case *serenity*. I devised for myself to take one day a week, and on that day to give no one any unsolicited advice.

Who knows whether this is true, but my hypothesis is that we're put here to learn certain lessons. We undergo a number of lifetimes, life experiences, and in the course of these lives we get to be different Enneagram styles, different genders, and probably a lot of other things that are different: the physical bodies we get to live in, different kinds of vocations. And we're put here to learn whatever it is we're meant to learn in that cycle. I'm not sure we even necessarily need to know what it is, or know that we've learned it. If we don't learn it this time around we'll be brought back in at least as challenging a situation that will force us to learn the same thing. And we'll have to keep going around until we learn it. Then there gets to be some peace, some serenity. You are the drop in the ocean and you dissolve and become the ocean.

So for each of us there is a path. The Enneagram is an amazing tool for coming to understand the terrain. You have to go out and struggle against your circumstances, your environment, everything you come into this world to be in the middle of, and having this map of the terrain can make it a little bit easier to fight the battles you have to fight. I wouldn't be able to lay out my own path for you. It's extremely complex. In a sense the task for all of us is learning to love unconditionally, in our different ways and with our different barriers to that.

The One says *Unless I'm right and good I cannot either love or be loved*, and this is not true, of course. The One says *I'm going to perfect the world*, and the little voice inside says *Wait a minute, maybe it's perfect as it is*. If I do put out a program for myself, it is to be able to be more kind to people. And *kindness*, maybe, means something different than it would have meant to me in the past. It doesn't necessarily mean helping them persist in their follies. It may just mean backing away and offering love without trying to get in their way.

But we don't exactly know where our paths lead until we get there, and I think trying to lay out a program for one's own path is arrogant, pretentious, and self-important. Basically, I don't think we have a clue until maybe the end when we get there. Or don't. There are moments, perhaps, of awareness. I've been given many gifts to help me learn things I'm glad to have learned. Whether any of those was *the* thing, I don't know.

Everything Has Sanctity – Kevin's Story

To me, transformation is part of my growth process as a person, not modifying what's there but giving up what was and putting the pieces together in a completely different fashion. It means surrendering, giving up what I felt was important before. And it's a journey in fits and starts. I can get bogged down. Usually, I'm already down the road before I realize, *Oh, that's what that was all about!* And that's one of the beauties of it: if you function in the here-and-now you aren't cognizant of change. We don't have to know and we really *don't* know, because if we spend all our time thinking, *Gee, what does this mean? What will happen if I do this*? then we thwart ourselves from actually doing something.

Coming into this openness was a revelation for me. I wasn't even aware of it until my children said, "Hey, Dad, you're different!" Then I reflected on it and realized, *Yeah, I am different.* I frame these changes in terms of being an Enneagram One, the acceptance of less than my vision of perfection. I'm more open about myself and more open to listening vs. pontificating. And with that, and probably more pertinent to showing myself and being available, is to acknowledge the worth of people.

This goes back to my upbringing, because to excel was expected. That was not because of superior background as far as family position or wealth. My father was a tailor and my mother a cook. I spent the first six years of my life – besides at home – living with my mother in the house where she was a domestic. I saw the fruits of success. They were mine to enjoy to some extent, because the people my mother worked for thought I was a nice little boy. At the same time I'd be helping my mother polish furniture. When I was nine to ten years old we spent two summers in Vermont, where my Mom and Dad were the summer help for a couple of spinster sisters who ran a boarding school and whose relatives would occasionally visit. Some of their grandkids were my age. They wanted to play and I wanted to play, but I was supposed to be cutting grass. I was a little bit ticked off at that, that I couldn't play with the other kids, but at the same time I remember an off-hand comment from one of the members of the family, "What the hell is he doing here?" So that was a wake-up call: *Oh, you really are different.* That's been pertinent throughout my life.

I was an only child and the community around me was mostly Slavic. Hungarian domestics. We lived in New Jersey and worked in a town of wealthy people. So we'd have a big crowd at the house on Thursdays and Sundays, which was the day off for my relatives. The family environment was very rich, very European. We had lots of extended family and it was wonderful, except that my father died when I was 12. By the time I was 14 years old my mother was deferring to me. I was the "man," which made me grow up quickly. Fortunately a new kid moved into the area when I was 16 or 17 and I latched onto his father. My friend would be off with other guys and I'd hang around with his dad, who in retrospect was a surrogate father. It was very helpful for me, and my mother supported it, so there wasn't any conflict.

Looking back over my life, the most significant change has been allowing myself to come out of my shell and, consequently, letting other people in. I was very much a child of the fifties in my marriage. I was duty-bound and decided I'd made my bed and was going to sleep in it. In that way I was a good father and a good husband. But in other ways I was probably a bad father and especially a bad husband, because I was very anxious to change my wife into what I thought the business person's wife should be. I had no idea what I was talking about, but there were examples that appealed to me. My wife wasn't that, and she still isn't. The way she dressed, and her value system is so right and it's never changed, but it wasn't the value system I saw in the wives of my business associates, the ones who were getting ahead. From where I can see now, it was superficial nonsense, and my wife didn't want any part of it. She hung in, she outlasted me! Our favorite saying now is, "Divorce, never; murder, yes!"

I changed to her side of the fence, and some of that is taking the time to look at this woman I was living with and realizing, *She's right!* Her journey started probably 25 years before mine did, so I'm playing real catch-up ball. Something in me finally surrendered. But there was an interim period where it was really rough for her, because my reaction was, *If you won't change, to hell with you.* I was always a sales person, and I inherited a job from a guy who was retiring. Wanting to change my wife had its genesis before then, but really came into focus at that point. There was a period of time when I seriously considered moving to the wealthier part of town, but it never came about because the kids were all in school and when we thought about it even slightly seriously, we said, "Let's wait until the kids are out of grammar school. Let's wait until..." So it never came about.

If we had made the move, I would have had to associate with the movers and shakers but work on a day-to-day basis with the guys in the mill. By keeping my distance geographically I could manage both ends very well. But this was a time when my wife chose not to change and I excluded her from most of my activities. I took great pains, from a business point of view, to look at *Where could she fit? Where could she be helpful?* And then slowly, over time, *Where would she enjoy being?* I was starting to consider her.

Like most changes, I've looked over my shoulder and said, *Oh, is that what that was all about?* I don't remember consciously making that effort at the time. Being purposeful is not something I've done except in the past ten years. That was triggered when I became president of the company I'd joined in 1979. Then in 1989 the company we primarily represented canceled our contract and hired our two best salesmen to work for them. So I quickly lost 75% of my income, which gave me food for thought. I assumed the *biblical sparrow* approach to life. *They're clothed and they're fed, we'll make it.* I ceased to be concerned about our financial future.

My wife probably helped save my sanity and also got me onto a whole different track, put a different purpose into my life: to consciously be about my own spiritual development, my own journey. There were fits and starts, and I don't know when the real transformation began. I know the groundwork was being laid for a long period of time, but it took me a hell of a long time to get into a posture of surrender instead of, "Yes, but..."

The area that comes to mind, especially, is the conscious effort to be open with my wife and my kids, an active emotional participant. That meant my expression of gratitude, of happiness, of joy in them. That was foreign to them, I'm sure, because I'd never done it. There was a little voice inside saying, *Quit screwing around, playing games and withholding yourself. Be real!*

I don't think you can organize a primer and say, "These are the steps to accepting yourself and others as you are and this is how it will happen." Because you have to surrender to your life experiences, and that takes patience, so that they'll fit into the new jigsaw puzzle you're putting together. Not having to fix everything means it will happen in its own good time if you give it a chance.

It's a paradox that the only way for me to transform is to be in the here-and-now, to not have to fix myself or anyone else. And that's the fun of it, to listen, to absorb, to give up, to have the patience to wait until a thing matures, and then to have the pleasure of looking over your shoulder and saying, *Oh!* And there's no end to it, it's constantly changing. What I thought was an *Oh!* six months ago I may or may not think is an *Oh!* anymore. To offer a formula for change is abhorrent to me. To offer a how-to-do book might be fine in business practices, but it's no way to live a life, because peoples' experiences are different. Every view is a point of view, and if I don't have a landing field to accept what you're saying, you may as well not have said it. Or if you've said it and it lands on the wrong landing field, I have a completely different response from what was intended.

Joseph Campbell influenced my more universal thinking, my openness, the importance of myth and metaphor in our lives. It's really freeing because I can accept the universality of all life and the sanctity of all life. It put a big exclamation point, beyond what I had already come to conclude, that my religion or my faith doesn't have a corner on truth at all. Other influences on me were generally associated with religiosity – workshops, retreats, and so forth. I functioned for about 25 years in the Lutheran church at the state level, with responsibilities on the executive board of the Lutheran Church of America. I've been privy to seven or eight national conventions, and have seen the feet of clay and the good stuff simultaneously. That gave me perspective.

Recently I had an atrial fibrillation and was in the hospital for cardiac conversion, which is electric shock with paddles, to get *re-booted*, like a computer. Fibrillation is when the top part of the heart is not in synch with the bottom part of the heart. During the cardiac conversion, the cardiologist zapped me three times with the maximum dosage. When I woke up and heard the monitor, the first words out of my mouth were, "Oh, shit!" Because I was still fibrillating. They took me back to my room and when I was alone I prayed. The extent of my prayer was, *What do You want me to do with this now?* Then, believe it or not, in about 2½ hours my doctors came shouting into the room saying, "You've converted!" I was back to sinus rhythm, which happens sometimes but, in retrospect, what came out of that for me was knowing it wasn't a prayer of pissing and moaning, of *Oh, isn't this awful! You didn't do right by me.* It wasn't bargaining; it was a sincere question: *What am I supposed to do with this now? How do You want me to use this?*

One of the authors I enjoy is Andrew Greeley, who chats on a daily basis with God. For Lutherans, prayer is a relationship with God, who loves you regardless. There's no condition in which you're not loved. Period. You can't do anything to stop that except to turn your back on Him. If you walk away, you walk away. But as long as you're there, we believe there is a relationship, and the *work*, anything you do, is not out of a sense of *should*, but to say, *Thank you.*

A vignette comes to me about this *patience* thing. There was a college reunion about 20 years ago. I didn't go, but filled out a five-page questionnaire. On the first run-through my answers were automatic, and there was one question very near the end, "What is the most important thing you have learned since leaving the university?" When I re-read it I got to this question at the end and thought, *Well, I'll be damned.* There were a lot of lines to fill in, but I had put one word: *patience.* That was it. I think that was a wake-up call. That was the first time I consciously gave it any thought. I was in my fifties.

I had spent forty years driving at least 30,000 miles and I was an aggressive driver. By that I mean if I was going to turn into the next lane, instead of falling behind somebody I'd speed up and go in front of them. And if there was someone driving like a yahoo in front of me, I'd get in front of them instead of having to worry about what they were going to do. And I didn't like people who are self-pitying, who are phony, who enlist sympathy when there's nothing sympathetic about their position. That would cause me anger. When my kids said I'd changed, that change was away from being critical and not expressing gratitude for something well done. And I guess part of that change is also the freedom of emotion, open emotion – showing my love, and exposing myself as well.

Yes, it's definitely being in the here-and-now, it's definitely overcoming ego, realizing *I am not the most important thing in the world*. Everything, the total creation, has sanctity in its own place.

Commentary

The overused gift of Style One is to be perfect. It's the Ego's way of attracting attention. And theirs is a great gift: who is perfect is really somebody! The two stories in this chapter illustrate what can happen when people of Style One move beyond the story Ego is telling. When they transform the need to be perfect into something much more.

In these stories, transformation is part of one's growth process as a person or an evolution of consciousness. There's a shift not only in the person, but also in the understanding of the idea of transformation. Each of these shifts helps relax the Ego's control, so more of the innate can emerge in their lives. For Alison, the Enneagram reinforces the idea that our personality, fixations and preoccupations are like garments we can put on – or take off.

A common trait of people of Style One is the need to fix themselves and others. This is part of Ego's story of trying to be perfect. Alison's experience of relaxing Ego came through a series of what Gurdjieff labels as shock points. One of these was learning about the Enneagram and a dawning awareness of its implications for her own life. Before this she had assumed everyone had the same perception as she did of right and wrong, of what it takes to be good,. It hadn't occurred to her that others might have a different focus of attention. This opened her to the question, "If I could be so mistaken about the way the world is, could I not be mistaken about a great many other things?"

In moments when the Ego relaxes, people of Style One can experience the virtue of *Serenity*, which Jerry Wagner describes as a "felt sense of integrity and completeness, a felt sense of ourselves as being good. Serenity exists when we trust others and their process, and when we trust the uninterrupted, uninterfered with unfolding of the universe." Kevin sees this as allowing himself to come out of his shell and, consequently, letting other people in. For Alison, it is to give no one any unsolicited advice.

Kevin describes his Ego armor in terms of wanting to fix others, of being judgmental. His story charts the profound moments that helped to rob this need of its strength. It provides beautiful examples of how, when Ego is relaxed, a person of Style One can experience the higher quality of *Acceptance*, an "acceptance of less than my vision of perfection. I'm more open about myself and more open to listening vs pontificating. And with that, and probably more pertinent to showing myself and being available, is to acknowledge the worth of people."

The gradual acceptance of his wife as she is, rather than the Stepford automaton he tried to make her, helped to save his sanity and injected a different purpose into his life, namely to be about his own spiritual development, his own journey.

Today, Alison and Kevin describe in similar ways how they move beyond the story their Egos are telling, illustrating a healthy sense of perspective of their role in the grand scheme of things. When in the here-and-now, Kevin realizes he's not the most important thing in the world. Everything has sanctity in its own place. Out of this springs the importance of developing and deepening the experience of patience in his life – the most important thing he learned since university.

When Alison transcends her Ego's need to perfect the world, a little voice says, *Wait a minute, maybe it's perfect as it is*. Out of this comes an ability to be more kind to others. Sometimes this kindness just means backing away and offering love without trying to get in the other person's way. "We don't exactly know where our paths will lead until we get there, and I think trying to lay out a program for one's own path is arrogant, pretentious and self-important. Basically, I don't think we have a clue until maybe the end when we get there. Or don't. There are moments, perhaps, of awareness. I've been given many gifts to help me learn things I'm glad to have learned. Whether any of these was *the* thing, I don't know."

Both Kevin and Alison illustrate the power of transformation in a person of Style One.

Three questions to ponder:

- How do I experience the need to fix others and from where does this spring forth?

- What is my life's work?

- When did I last accept myself as I am?

Contents

1. Breaking Down the Illusions – Jessica's story   21

2. Staying Awake – Bryan's story   30

3. Commentary   36

Chapter Two – Style Two

Breaking Down the Illusions – Jessica's story

The word *transformation* means getting back to my *self*. It's not so much changing who I am, it's *finding* who I am. I've gone through many big transformations in my life – changes in lifestyle, the way I look at things, the way I act, the way I feel, but it's more letting go of the parts that weren't me. And that's much harder than meets the eye. Thirty years ago, when I first started this, I would have had many more answers than I do today!

As an Enneagram Two, meeting my needs is much more difficult than meeting other peoples' real or supposed needs. At first, I couldn't as easily see where I was giving myself away. When I consciously started meeting my needs, I also began to see I was giving too much energy to other peoples' needs; I could clearly see where I was giving myself away. For example, when I started an art business and spent much more time in my art work and in solitude, *then* I could see my marriage was lopsided; I was giving much more energy than I was getting back from it. As I started to take care of myself in my marriage, my former husband became more and more depressed and mentally ill, because I was taking energy away. In retrospect after the divorce – because I felt so good – I knew what had happened. But until I started taking better care of myself in the marriage I couldn't see what I was doing. I wasn't aware of it.

For me the self-care needs were basic solitude needs. Every day at sunset I'd would walk to a hill in the cemetery and watch the sunset, then walk back to the little town I lived in. I started my art business at the same time, so I was spending many hours a day alone at painting. And that got me in touch with the rest of my life that I hadn't seen because I was in it so hard. Just making myself do those things I knew were right to do – in my case food or exercise or solitude issues – became a little window to help me clearly see the bigger picture, that I was not living healthfully and really not in a good place with relationships.

On a larger scale, I recognized the dysfunction in my marriage of choosing someone who needed my energy because it made *me* feel OK. But when I spent four years with a second man and he literally went insane when we broke up – the same as my former husband – that was one of the biggest aha's in my life: *You look like you're well, you look like you're functioning much better, you're taking good care of yourself, you didn't marry this person, but it's the very same thing you did before.* I'd again chosen someone who needed my energy, needed me in order to survive, so I would feel good. And seeing that pattern repeated was *huge* for me, just a *huge* thing!

The other thing that's helped me transform is being able to seize opportunities intuitively. Even when I wasn't always aware of it, I would do things that were good for me at the right time, just from intuition. For example, 25 years ago I lived in this tiny town, where an early writer about human potential was born. I was reading every book I could find at that time and one winter I got all the powers that be in that little town to my house and said, "I think we need to invite him to this town." So the next summer they did, and I had an autograph party for him at my house. After that party he told me, "You can't let yourself get sick from your husband's mental illness." And I started crying because I thought, *How did he know that? I haven't told that to anyone.* Probably anyone with insight would have seen it, but because I hadn't talked about it I wasn't aware it was visible. Then he told me he was having this workshop the next summer in Montana, called the *School of Life*, and I said "I'll be there." So I called three friends and said, "I think we need to go to this workshop" and they said, "What is it about?" and I said, "I don't know," but the four of us drove to Montana not knowing what it was going to be. And that was one of the first huge therapy sessions I'd had that was really useful to me. It really started to break down the illusions.

The following summer I went again, and then the next year I was able to walk out of my marriage and get my divorce. That therapy helped me, because I'd had messages that if I left he'd commit suicide, it was important to keep my promises, the children needed a two-parent home, etc.

The precipitating events in my life were huge events that also brought big feelings. I started to look at events at that time as neither good nor bad. For example, my younger brother died at 42 and I went into grieving that was inappropriate for the event. Because I couldn't stop grieving, I realized it went deeper, and that got me into some real heavy-duty therapy. So, precipitating events have always been positive even if the event seemed negative. I've stopped looking at events as positive or negative. I look at whatever it is, all there to help me with what I came here to learn.

When I found the Enneagram I thought, *Oh my goodness! These are the issues I've been in therapy about, that I've worked and worked and worked on, and here they are in a book!* That's why I thought, *This is like a magic thing that could have helped me!* I'm not sure I would have read it at an earlier age, but it would have been helpful had I read it. I could have seen the dynamics more clearly and perhaps not repeated them as many times in colossal ways.

With the second lover, the man after my marriage, my back started hurting one summer and physically I knew there was something wrong with the relationship, but I didn't know it yet mentally. Had I known the Enneagram at that time, I would have been able to ask myself some questions that would have helped me. And I wouldn't have had to wait until my leg started hurting and I maybe would have seen more clearly and closed the relationship off sooner.

It's also helped me to understand the part about being indispensable. Some views of the Two are about the dependence part. But my subtype, the counter-subtype, the social subtype, is very independent. I tried to be all for everything, to be indispensable. So after I quit men and said, *I've got to get healthier so I don't keep doing this* and went into therapy again – around relationships and my own identity as a woman – then I made myself indispensable to a whole company and practically burned out physically over that.

So with my former husband, my mother, and the company, there were three times when my personality nearly killed me physically. Had I not gotten out of it I could have easily gotten sick and died from it. The work addiction and the whole energy high of being indispensable was so alluring and such a habit, I couldn't see I was getting tired and, because I hadn't slept for so many years, I was physically starting to burn out. I couldn't see that. Luckily we had a buy-out, so I quit, then went into this real, real slump. It was diagnosed as chronic fatigue syndrome, but I think it was burn-out. I think I was just exhausted from putting that much energy out for that many years. And the *pride* about that! My view was *Other people need sleep. I don't!* So I knew how to get my wants met, I thought my self-esteem was building so I could get my *wants* met, and I did, but I didn't get my *basic* needs met. I was stuck in a different way!

At that time I started intervening with the needy part of myself. Because of the Enneagram, I consciously stopped being indispensable in relationships – with family, with lovers, in the workplace. But instead of giving accurate help to the part of me that was healing, the small child that needed help inside of me, I started intervening with my *personality*. For example, I'd feel lonely and eat ice cream at night, instead of journaling and doing the crying and other things I knew to do. My ego, my *type* would intervene by giving that person what I thought she needed, which wasn't really what she needed at all! Or I'd go shopping. This was a little bit like Nines doing *narcotization*, but more keeping that needy child quiet, vs. letting the pain of it come out. So when I did this big alone time, took a year and a half off and just did walking and my art work in my studio, I really thought I was healing but I see now that I got back into food addiction. At the time I couldn't see it. I thought I was doing good work, and I'm not saying I wasn't. I think it was good work to withdraw from the other things I'd always done, but I was *still* doing the personality.

I don't "awfullize" this as much as I used to. It's all part of the process. Lately I've been looking at my spiritual life, whether it's meditation or quiet or living in the moment, as a way to build power internally in my *real* self. And when I do that my drive toward personality is lessened.

I do this in several ways. I've worked on a meditation practice that is now part of my life every day. It took me seven years with a group to do that. Because I'm so relational and so into groups, it helps me to get a group together to do it. So I started a meditation group and we met for seven years every single week for two hours and never missed. That gave me a shot every Sunday morning, to help me through the week, to get my own practice going. I'm also doing qigong a little bit every day, not as long as I'd like to, but at least it's going, and I journal. For years I've done walking but for about the last three or four years not every day, so I'm getting that going again. My artwork is a big thing, a mirror for my internal process that can help me see it much more easily than I otherwise can.

At one time I started painting angels, far from what I would have chosen to do, because I'm a trained artist and like nonobjective artwork. But I had to paint these angels, would go to my studio and paint angels for days and they would speak to me. It was a *very* holy thing. I didn't know how to get *out* of it, didn't know it was really like being at a meditation retreat for three days. So I'd go out shopping, go out to dinner, go to a concert and I'd get sick! Then I realized I had to come out of it the way I would have if it were a retreat. So when I painted for days in a row in that kind of space I had to just be quiet when I got home, eat lightly, and slowly get back into the world again.

That's how powerful the painting is. It evokes healing mood and is also healing because looking at the work I can see my inner process. When I got into dealing with some strong guilt I painted these dark, many-layered, kind of thick paintings. And when I stopped doing the angels I did a whole series of spirals. I had a whole show of spirals. A teacher I've had said, "These are about transition, spiraling you out into the next phase of your life."

Right now I'm doing this wonderful thing called Visual Journaling. I'm doing drawings and then writing and speaking with the drawings. So I'm taking that angel-speak that happened on its own to a much more deliberate level. When I have a question, I can do a drawing going into the space of the question, and then by dialoguing with the drawing later I can get the answer.

I have collages I've put up that have spiritual images in the center, and then I make a wheel so the symbols of the other parts of my life are on the outside of the wheel. And every time I've made those, every single thing on them comes true, not always within a year, but within a period of time.

In the last three years or so, it's been a combination of clearing and a statement. I would have quiet, then I'd bring myself back to a statement that's called up, like a truth. I got those statements from a teacher, but I've also developed my own. For the seven years I worked with that group I did Anthony de Mello's *Sadhana*. For years I did the statement *God loves me, I love myself*. I was traveling on the road in those years, and I would sing it in the car for hours. I used the statement as an affirmation except that I'd sing it. Then one day I could feel it take hold. It moved from my head and my voice down into my belly. And I just started weeping. It was like a page turned. Now when my mind starts wandering again I say *God loves me*.

The other thing that's really helpful to me is the Observer, just watching without judging how often the personality comes in. I'd say I notice it at least every half hour.

Another Two said "I thought of myself as always riding on this big horse, and I could do anything and go anywhere. Then one day I realized the horse was deciding where we were going." When I stopped work and decided to take some time off and really find myself, I got off the horse, and found myself so very vulnerable, so little, and I'd always felt so big. Then when I was ready to get back on the horse, the horse was so little! I had this tiny little horse, and I felt so vulnerable without that personality, without reaching out, making friends and getting support and being liked by people. I finally decided to ride on a spirit horse. In my mind's eye I saw this big blue horse, and that's the horse I try to ride on now.

I started doing work with mothers and daughters and had them bring something of their mothers'. Then I had them name their lineage, and we invited all those ancestors to stand around the circle as we did our work. The feeling was just amazing. Part of it was the grounding of those objects, and then the calling in of the spirits. So I think my work will have to do with some of these things because the journaling and the visual things I've done have really been helpful to me – very, very helpful.

Along with the events I've intuitively chosen to do, my spiritual life has moved along on its own. The path has been laid out in front of me. I've been to many workshops. One that stands out as life changing was in Hawaii. Before that, I was still working at being indispensable, trying to be there for someone else. We did an experience around money, where we could join a $100 group, a $50 group, a $20 group, a $10 group, or a $5 group. We put the money in, and then whoever was unanimously voted by the group to get the money would get the money from the group. There were ten in my group who had each put in a $100, a $1000 total. We each said what we wanted to do with this money and the person who won had a clear intention about what he was going to do. I said, "I know I'm going to do my thing," but I couldn't speak the intention clearly enough that the other people got it. In fact, the intention I had at that time is finally coming to fruition now. Before that time, I hadn't realized my intention wasn't strong enough to be spoken.

Another workshop was at Esalen – where I went on a backpack trip for seven days. Both were exactly what I needed to do next at that time in my life. So I seize opportunities and I've also structured a very strong support system for myself. I did not get emotional support in my marriage, so I had to find good support. I then was able to develop that skill, so I do know how to get good support.

And I've learned how to measure energy, so I sense if someone is taking too much energy in my life and I don't let that happen. For example, if I have dinner or go to an event with someone and I feel worse afterwards, I know I gave too much energy and didn't get enough back. I just measure how I feel, and if I'm drained, or feel less energetic then I know that person is taking energy. This has been a big learning, because for years I was so tickled to be connected to someone I'd let them take energy even if I was drained. I needed those connections so much. Now I make it a conscious effort to get good support from people. It's not just gathering friends; it's gathering the support I need. I set up a team in my company where I would get a lot of affirmation for years. At first I would weep when I got affirmations. Then later I could receive them and not weep. And then I didn't need them in order to be OK. And pretty soon I could do something and I didn't need anybody to say anything – I knew if it was good or wasn't, or useful or wasn't useful. I could be much more objective. But setting up that network, building a system of being loved and affirmed helped me get a strong enough base that I could pull forward.

The other thing is truth-telling. I work very diligently daily on telling the truth. I have a very strong pull to exaggerate, to make myself look better than I am, to only tell the good news, and so I'm watchful about that. I try to even watch my language. I don't say, "Well, to tell you the truth…" In other words, I don't try to set that apart and unique. I try to make everything truthful.

I've associated it with being a Two, trying to look good, trying to be perceived as being of value. I don't exaggerate in my work as much as in small things about who I am. For example, I was at a party one night and I met this man from Morocco who had traveled the entire world. I was very interested in hearing all about it, and I knew I'd never see him again, so when he asked me where I'd traveled overseas I said I'd been to London twice; which was truthful, and then it was all I could do not to say I'd been to Paris. I've never been to Paris. I thought somehow I would seem less boring if I said, "I've been to Paris, too!" When I think of that, it seems absurd to me. What do I care! What would he care? Nobody cared! It was just my habit, a habit I now have to really watch.

Looking back over my life, I don't even know myself. I'm unrecognizable except for my facial features. In fact, I went back to a town where I lived 30 years ago, and the woman I was visiting had some of my old friends over for coffee. I sat at the table and thought *I don't fit with these people anymore! These used to be my friends!* I must have been very different, because everything they said I either didn't agree with or didn't understand. Either I'd say something and shock them, or I'd have to hold my tongue and not say anything. So my presentation of who I am in the world is so different that I don't fit with old friends.

See, Twos can fit into any situation. What was different is that I made a choice in some cases to not say what I thought because of the shock of it. But it wasn't because I wanted to fit in, it was because I was being polite to the hostess, wasn't going to start a controversy – which wouldn't have served a purpose at that point. It was a choice rather than the habit I used to have of altering so I fit the situation. What I did say, I could see on their faces, was shocking. And I also was obvious with silence at times. I just couldn't say anything. There was so much altering that I even knew at the time I was altering. I knew I was different at different events with different people. So then to really try to be authentic, to be really who you are all the time is very different from any of those other people.

After my brother died, I would cry for months. As I get more into it, there's much more joy, but the pain is much deeper and much harder. Now I try to deal with the pain every day. It's so deep and so thick that it feels like regurgitating. It feels like gagging and choking on it. It's the exact same kind of body feeling I would be having if I were throwing up.

There's a psychiatrist who said we all have sludge at the bottom. Every time we get stirred up, that sludge comes up and we're murky inside. And if we want clarity, we have to get the sludge out. The more I get that sludge cleared out, the joy is much higher, life is much easier, and my intuition is much stronger – I just *know* stuff. But that sludge is *huge*, and this winter I came into this big, big, big, big pocket of it. And I probably could have done that five years earlier if I hadn't been intervening – with TV and food and movies and activities and different things I would do to quiet it. I'm not saying that's wrong. I think you have to do what you can do when you're ready. But I also know that the last seven years, when I've been consciously working on stopping the personality, have been the hardest seven years of my life. It's just digging in its heels, just stubborn and *real* willful. That good church lady feels like she's dying now, and she doesn't want to.

Chapter Two

I think there's a higher power directing the opportunities. They were always laid out right there for me and I was then able to seize them. I have diligently sought out what I needed. My spiritual quest started when I was very little, and was kind of derailed into Christianity for a while. For years I was running around in my personality, right there in the church and working diligently for spirituality, but I never was home and I didn't know it. I think of the Enneagram as helping me to be home so I can be there when the spirit speaks.

Staying Awake – Bryan's Story

To me *transformation* is becoming anew. It's also realizing potentials. Certainly it's changing from where you are or have been to a new place, a positive change, beginning to realize potentials that were already built into you when you came into the world.

Going to medical school was a transforming experience. It taught me how to become more analytical, to set myself apart from circumstances and view them third person in an objective way. I'd had several experiences as an orderly in a hospital where I'd get weak-kneed at the sight of blood, so one of my greatest concerns was passing out in the anatomy lab. This didn't go away immediately but, as I treated patients through medical school and residency, I was able to distance myself somewhat, take personalized feelings out, and more objectively assess what needed to be done at the time.

Another transforming experience for me has been my wife's mental illness, which has revealed to me the nature of humanness in general, and particularly my own humanness, as I see it reflected in her illness. It reminds me of a story in medicine about a Canadian trapper who accidentally shot himself in the stomach. He was out in the wilderness and got medical care in a fairly primitive setting. As a result, he ended up with a large fistula between his stomach and his abdominal wall, so researchers were able to observe what happened; for example, feeding him something and seeing acid produced. That's a close analogy for my wife's illness. She's a multiple personality, so she's divided into several persons, with certain functions and feelings relegated to each. And to see how all that interacts is like looking into the stomach and seeing what happens when certain stimuli go in.

Being with her has changed me. I'm more sensitive to individuals and how they respond to different stimuli. Part of this comes from the reading her illness has spawned. Books about multiple personality include personality development in general, which gives me more insight into what makes us who we are. I've also read Scott Peck and others who focus on how we become who we are. It's been challenging to understand the nature of this disease, and why she does certain things.

My biggest struggle has been balancing a core value of commitment or obligation with getting my needs met. Many of my emotional and social needs are unmet through the marriage. Both sexual intimacy and other forms of intimacy are highly sensitized through flashbacks for my wife. Certainly sexual intimacy is highly stigmatized for her. It's as though her sexuality has been obliterated. Emotional intimacy is also difficult for her. A book that's meant a lot to me is *Love and Survival*. The author, Dean Ornish, is a physician who writes clinically about the impact of lack of intimacy on physical health. People get sick and are more likely to die without intimacy and connectedness in their lives. And my wife was unable to read the book. That kind of intimacy – knowing another, being vulnerable at that level of trust – was very threatening to her. She has strong alters who block anything that seems to threaten them.

When this all erupted on the scene, I was told, "Well, in six months to a year things will start getting better." But we've been down several routes of taking her to specialists, to a specialty center, adding people to her therapy team, doing googobs of therapy. That has also served to support wishful thinking about what might be, and as time passes it's more and more difficult to support that kind of hope. Then it comes down to, *What needs do I have that can never be met in this relationship? Do I look at meeting my own needs and leaving the relationship?*

This is also very frustrating for my wife because she'd like to meet my needs but is just unable to. At times we've come close to agreeing both of us might be better off if we were separated. Some aspects in our relationship probably promote her remaining ill instead of getting better. She goes to three therapists for six to eight hours of therapy a week. One of the therapists suggested all this therapy has kept the *status quo* going. She's not had to go in the hospital for several years and she's been functional day-to-day, keeping house, cooking, taking care of the kids, and other things she likes. I've learned to not make demands she can't meet. This all creates a protective environment that allows her to be disintegrated as an individual, yet maintain what to most people from the outside looks like a normal life.

We were coming to some kind of resolution, but that was at the most difficult time in my life, when I was dealing with the stresses of my last job and making the transition to this one. It was too much change in too little time, more than I could deal with. The guy I used to work for did unspeakable things to me a couple of times. He belittled me at the beginning of a meeting in front of the whole leadership team. My staff was appalled. He didn't have an appreciation for the people side of the business. I'm feeling more relaxed with this job change. I love what I'm doing, it feels right, and I've paid close attention to positioning myself where I really want to be.

I feel anxious, however, knowing I'm down to the conflict between staying and leaving my marriage. And at times I've had to confront myself about staying for my benefit and to her detriment. There are obviously financial issues to leaving. Then there's worrying *What will people think?* Hardly anyone identifies her as being as ill as she is. She masks it so well that to outward appearances she's a nice, pleasant, quiet person. People might say, "He must be some liar, making all this stuff up."

Through coaching I've realized what intimacy is for me and what potentials may not be realized in this marriage. A lot of that has come from greater awareness of my own needs and at least an idea of how my needs could be met. And I've expanded my capacity for other emotionally intimate, nonsexual relationships where at least I can get some of my intimacy needs met. I've allowed myself to experience affection with other women, and some intimate relationships with men. So even though sexual intimacy needs can't be met, I've identified two things: I am capable of close relationships and it can happen with other people.

Those were important steps for me to take, because I could recognize and move through some of the negative dynamics that came from being married to my wife. The objectivity I developed while becoming a physician allowed me to stay in the marriage early on. We had severe problems in the middle of my medical training, and I became practiced at denying myself intimacy. So these recent experiences opened the door to a feeling of what intimacy could be like. One relationship was with a nurse I worked with, who revealed she'd grown up in a home with emotional abuse. And I told her some of my past, particularly the difficulties in my relationship with my wife. She's a psych nurse who knows quite a bit about multiple personality. Then my father had a stroke. In pretty short order I had to get on a plane, see what was going on, and make arrangements to move him back here. I was afraid he'd die and I wouldn't be there, and this nurse came over and put her hands on my back. The sensation was different than anything I'd ever felt before – a very caring and loving touch – and I broke down and cried, which I'd rarely done in any circumstance. It was genuine and meant a lot to me.

I recognize now I was attracted to and stayed with my wife in the early part of our marriage because I had a need to avoid intimacy at that point. It made me feel good to be able to be a caregiver, to have someone in need to take care of and provide for.

With 360 feedback two years ago, the response came out that I was willing to help others but didn't allow others to help me. I'd been the Big Daddy on the team, making sure everybody got along, helping to resolve all the conflicts. That was the first time I was exposed to the notion of the negative aspects of caretaking. I came to realize how I'd used caretaking as a means of controlling others. That triggered a lot of self-evaluation, self-exploration for me, and led to much of the reading and subsequent work I've done. I still have that summary report, and every once in a while I pull it out and re-read it, to remind myself where I've been and where I am now.

I recently read Scott Peck's *A World Waiting to be Reborn* where he writes about *false civility*. To him, civility is not being artificially nice or patronizing but being honest and genuine in a relationship, whether it's a marriage, or work, or whatever. And I've begun to think about that, to improve on what I've considered my role of being the *go-between* but at times sacrificing honesty for peace. Peck pointed out that you have to work to a point of trust where you can be honest and genuine, and then you can resolve whatever conflicts that produces. He says resolving conflict creates personal, spiritual growth. So you can mutually create spiritual growth in each other.

My reading on Western modes of meditation helped me conceptualize my connectedness to God, listening to the God within us. That voice is always there, the message and the wisdom, so it's learning how to be quiet enough to listen. A few times I've gotten wisdom from that voice, and those times have been marked by an incredible sense of peace and well-being and knowledge of what to do. It's very clear. You just *know*. I've had a very clear message from my inner voice, a series of four occasions spread out over several years, the last one about a year ago: *It's time to go, I have other work for you to do*. I struggled with actually following through on that and the follow-up message was, *Trust me*. It was that simple and plain

But I get discouraged, feel depressed, a sense of hopelessness, and recognize what I call *circling the drain* events, the same things all over again, same feelings, and same things going on in my life and getting nowhere, like when you pull the plug and the water's circling the drain. At times I normalize my marriage: things are cruising along, meals are on the table, Hi's and Goodbye's, and reasonably pleasant conversations. Then, wham, one of these bizarre things multiples are capable of will come out of the blue. It might be night terrors where I can't awaken my wife, or dreams she reveals, or she'll ask an incredibly naïve question. The most extreme is when an alter makes itself known.

That sometimes pulls me back into being the caretaker, I can't help it. For her as for many people, all her alters are small children in a great deal of pain, whimpering children probably three to four years of age. I'd feel cruel to not reach out. I want to hug her. But coincidental with that is the circling the drain feeling and I think, *Here I am again! Is this ever going to end or change in a substantial way?*

My woodworking continues to be a way of sorting things out. While I'm doing the work, things are processing. A lot of it I do without conscious thinking, but it's also extremely tactile, so it's a combination of being tactile and visual. Pretty soon I'm shaping more than an object and it's become a live metaphor for what I'm doing. Recently it's been very helpful for me to make things for other people: I think of that person and that relationship while I'm shaping what I'm working on. When I left my last job I took the four senior managers out to dinner and gave each of them a shaker box made of cherry wood, saying how I thought of them as I shaped and sanded and made this beautiful thing for each of them. It was very powerful for all of us.

I use the metaphor of a *journey* for all these changes. I used to think the journey was destination-specific, but now I realize it's life-long, a quest for understanding, deepening the spiritual ties, improving all kinds of relationships: with God, with myself, with others around me. And the purpose of life is to continue on the journey, not to get to some end point. I've had some real ups and downs, but I'm on an upswing. Scott Peck believes in marriage but also recognizes some marriages can be destructive. And if my wife and I continue to go through a good process, including lengthy introspection, I would accept it as a full possibility that she could be better because she is away from me and that could be the best thing for both of us. Right

Chapter Two

now I need more data before I can leave this marriage. We're still making progress on that part of the journey.

Commentary

The overused gift of Style Two is to be connected. It is their Ego's way of attracting attention. This great gift of theirs often takes the form of helping or giving. The two stories in this chapter illustrate what can happen when people move beyond the story their Egos are telling. When they transform the need to be connected into something much more.

In these stories transformation is seen as "becoming anew. It's also [...] beginning to realize potentials that were already built into you when you came into the world," as Bryan put it. For Jessica it's similar, "not so much changing who I am, it's *finding* who I am."

A common trait of people of Style Two is to either not recognize or underplay their own needs. This is part of Ego's story of striving to be connected: their energy pours into connecting with others, at the cost of neglecting to be connected with themselves. Jessica describes this as "always riding on this big horse, and I could do anything and go anywhere. Then one day I realized the horse was deciding where we were going." Her first experiences of relaxing Ego came through solitude, while either walking or painting. She charts the deepening experiences of relaxing Ego that solitude brings her.

In moments when the Ego relaxes, people of Style Two can experience the virtue of *Humility*, which Jerry Wagner calls the "reality principle. It acknowledges our limitations and boundaries and offers the [...] freedom to voice 'no' as well as 'yes'." Bryan describes this in his ongoing struggle in his marriage to balance the core value of commitment with getting his needs met.

He experiences his Ego armor as lack of connection to self. His story describes the deep moments in his marriage and work that weakened this lack of connection. He shows how, when Ego is relaxed, a person of Style Two can experience the higher quality of *Freedom*, which he describes as being "able to distance myself somewhat, take personalized feelings out, and more objectively assess what needed to be done at the time." This freedom is illustrated in how differently Bryan views life as a journey. Earlier it was destination-specific, today it is a life-long quest for understanding and deepening of the main relationships in his life: with God, himself and the people around him.

Jessica speaks of the sludge all of us have at the bottom. Every time we get stirred up, we get murky inside. The more she clears the sludge, the more joy, ease and intuition she experiences in her life.

Today, they describe in similar ways how they move beyond the story their Ego is telling. Jessica notices when someone is taking too much energy from her life, and focuses her attention instead on relationships that offer her good support. Bryan calls such energy sapping as "*circling the drain* events."

Another way these Style Two people move beyond their Ego's story is through art. Bryan uses woodworking to sort things out. When he makes an object for someone it helps him to review their relationship. Jessica's non-objective artwork evokes a healing mood and allows her to see her inner process. These times spent painting are like days in a retreat. As she says, "For years I was running around in my personality, right there in the church and working diligently for spirituality, but I never was home and I didn't know it. I think of the Enneagram as helping me to be *home* so I can be there when the spirit speaks."

Three questions to ponder:

- In what ways am I blind to my needs?

- How do I recognize when people are draining my energy?

- When did I last enjoy my contribution to what is?

Contents

1. The Seasons of our Lives – Grant's story   39

2. Level by Level – Valerie's story   48

3. Commentary   52

Chapter Three – Style Three

The Seasons of our Lives – Grant's story

All my life, until I started doing some real work, it was *how things look* as opposed to how I really am. *How do I appear outwardly*? It's like living a lie: *How do I fool people*? Image was really important. The image of how people saw me was more important than anything. I wasn't that conscious of it. Threes are very achievement oriented, very outer oriented. We're not in touch with what we feel. It's more what we look like, how we appear. So all the energy goes out to being a success, achieving and putting on a show, putting on a face you want others to see and hiding what's underneath – not even being aware of what's underneath. That's the basic pattern, like a peacock that struts around and shows off its feathers.

You're just not in touch with what's really authentic, because you're so covered up with the mask, it becomes what you think is real, what you think is authentic, but it's just a mask you're wearing. We're living in a Three culture – so you can see what goes on out there: achievement, and how things look.

I'd been a teacher and a coach and wasn't making enough money to support my family. I was in the exchange brokerage business, had a real estate office, and needed to make money in real estate to survive, so a couple of us got together and hired a therapist to help us learn how to sell. We met with him weekly, and what it boiled down to was that in order for me to know how people were responding to me I had to know about myself, to see what they were responding to. He was teaching us how to sell, how to relate to people, how to motivate people. Back then I realized I wasn't an aggressive kind of sales person. I wasn't someone who wanted to sell for selling's sake. I wanted to be a good guy. In retrospect my image was important, so I didn't want to appear like I was pushy. I had to develop a manner that didn't appear pushy because how people thought of me was important, it covered a lot of how I related.

But the bottom line was that I had to look at myself in order to do that, coming from the inside rather than applying a lot of techniques of selling on the outside. I had to learn more about who I was so I could come off in a more authentic way, be more believable to people and more trustworthy. That got me on the road to doing the inner work, started me on Gestalt and other therapies, to discover more of who I was. The comedy of the inner work was that it backfired, because then I didn't want to do the real estate business anymore. Working with that therapist was the beginning of transformation for me, the beginning of inner work, inner awareness. That's when I moved into Rolfing.

Going through divorce in the midst of all this study was transformative because it forced me to look at my patterns, my responses, how I dealt with my children through the separation. That was a major shock point. My work with Claudio Naranjo was very transformative, and the Fisher-Hoffman Quadrinity Work – where I looked at my parental patterns, reviewed my life, my history. They call it the Hoffman Quadrinity Process now. I went through the program and then became a teacher, taking groups through the process. Basically, you work from zero through puberty, looking at your negative patterns, things you don't like about yourself; then you look at your parents, your caregivers, and get the thread going through your life as you grow up and see where the patterns come from. Then at least you have a handle on it, and you can choose whether you want to keep it or not. It's powerful therapy. I think it takes a lot of years off of traditional therapy. The four components of the quadrinity are the body, intellect, emotions and spirit, and there's work in each of those areas.

Claudio tied the Fisher-Hoffman work to the Enneagram, and that gave me a clue as to where all these patterns came from. Those two major experiences got me on the road, more in touch with my internal process and working ongoing with the process.

Because of the inner work my goals changed somewhat. I became more conscious of my image, more conscious that what I did was important so I would still look good. I became a little more authentic, or at least I was able to play the game a little better so I would look good even though I was trying to push. It's been so long ago I can hardly remember what I was like then. Certainly image, achievement, athletics, and being out there in front were important. I'd been a football coach and a baseball coach. That was an achievement very early in my career and I got a really choice spot in a choice school. Being a good coach might be altruistic in itself, helping the students achieve something, but I think I went into coaching because it's out there in front – to get noticed, to have people say, "Oh, just look at that! He's a great guy!" That was the raw motivation. It was very exciting, challenging, frustrating. I loved being a leader, putting my ideas into practice. It was also an area where I could have self-doubt and pretend I didn't. I think Threes do that. We're arrogant in a lot of ways but underneath it is self-doubt, overcompensating for what we haven't enough of in our lives. For me it was being frightened and pretending I wasn't. Not knowing everything I thought I should know, because you never know enough so you're always striving to learn more.

I was inspirational and I think that's carried on to my life right now. I'm a minister and people comment that my lessons are inspirational. It's not really motivational, it's not a rah-rah thing anymore. Maybe at one time it was; maybe when I was coaching, but I think I was a little softer than that. Still, it was inspiring people toward doing what I wanted them to do!

It's difficult for me to talk about myself and my feelings. That's part of doubting myself. At this stage I'm learning more and more to accept the qualities I've developed. I don't think I had the awareness I have now. I'm becoming more assured of who I am, but I've spent a lot of work, a lot of time. I don't think I would naturally talk about my qualities.

I can take the Three patterns back to grammar school. I remember how important it was for me to look good – wanting to be accepted by my peers and look good. It didn't matter if I was good or not, I wanted to appear good. I can think of one incident where I was late for a baseball game we were playing and I rode up on my bike and everybody cheered and da da da da. I didn't know that I was that good. Maybe I was, but I never acknowledged myself as being that good. But everybody yelled and I said, *Yeah, I'm here!*

There was never enough assurance, and I still work on it. I don't know that you ever gain it. There are levels and levels of layers and layers that resurface. And attempting to be conscious of those patterns I've learned about myself, the Three qualities – and they do come up – I see it and can chuckle at it or respond differently, or say to myself, *Oh, that's what's going on* and get off it. The transformational process has allowed me in part to not act or behave in those ways as intensely as I once did, but certainly it's there. I don't know that we ever get through our fixation. I think the transformation process helps us become more aware, more conscious, so our behaviors and patterns change. But I think the fixation always remains with us.

Self-doubt was one of the patterns I learned about. I got the message that I was supposed to be good enough and smart enough to become a professional, a doctor, a lawyer, an accountant, or someone of that nature. But my parents discouraged me from studying a musical instrument, saying they'd spend money on lessons and I'd just quit, because I wouldn't be good enough. Yet something in me longed to play music at an early age. It was very conflicting for me to have that negative expectation put into me. To this day I still struggle trying to learn music, trying to fill that hole. That's the self-doubt, the message I got and grew up with: *I'm not good enough.*

I get frustrated, very frustrated. But I do continue. I keep striving and I usually achieve everything I try. But I'm still trying to prove I'm good enough and know enough. Even if it doesn't work, when I tackle something I keep trying to find ways to make it work. And I do get a result but it doesn't match the standard I carry. I'm still dealing with that, still trying to learn. It's such a deep desire for me to learn to play music. But I'm critical because I don't think I'm good enough, not spontaneous enough, not *enough*! And I put a lot of obstacles in my way rather than just getting up and playing three chords and making that OK. It's like I've got to be the best. It feels good when I can play along and sing a song, when I can learn new things, when I can perform. I don't want to be mediocre, to appear mediocre. I need to appear *good.* So I have to consciously make it OK to just be how I am with it. But it doesn't flow that way naturally.

Even at this point, not that I'm so enlightened, how I judge myself is probably the thing I need to stay conscious of most often. I judge myself way too much, way too intensely. I have to constantly do my little self-talk when that comes up. But I take more risks now, do things even though they might not be perfect, just do what I do. But it's not easy underneath. The feelings underneath don't feel solid or confident or secure. It doesn't flow naturally. I have to get the courage up, do the self-talk.

It's a lot better than it used to be. I have transformed in some way. I do more things from an easy place, and I'm generally pretty conscious of it. When I look back at it, I did the singing, the performance, to move through some of those inhibitions I had, some of those patterns. Then I created a whole work around it for others. What I taught was to feel the fear and do it anyway. To move through and let the experience teach you something different rather than what's in your head, or the patterns. So basically, that might be my credo right now. If I were going to suggest something for Threes – or anyone, actually – it would be to move through their pattern, to get right up to the edge and push it. And for me, performance and looking good is the edge. I've got to be willing to get out there and not look good. Or at least in my opinion not look good. I still might look good for others. But for me I might think I'm not good enough, might have doubts about it, and get away from the image of trying to look good and just do what I do.

I've always been a searcher, a gatherer, in spite of the self-doubt. And maybe the gathering was to try to compensate for the self-doubt. Somehow that drive was in me innately to gather techniques, information. I started meditation really early and that felt right for me, something I felt aligned with, had a hunger for, something innate, and it was nurtured by wanting to do it right. That moved me into more and more spiritual work.

The word *spiritual* means so many things. Back in those days it was being in touch with, aligning with some energy or power or God in some way. That's true for me today, too, just trusting and knowing this is a friendly universe, things happen and it's only our perception that makes them good or bad. Changing the way I think. Spirit is something within me and out there, too. It's a Gestalt.

I was very involved with Buddhist teachings for quite a while and still am, in a way. Some of the East Indian teachings I've studied have really helped me, and the work in seminary I did to become a minister, interpreting the bible metaphysically and how many of the events are part of our own lives. It's certainly been part of my transformation to work with different people, different teachers – Buddhist teachers, Jewish teachers, Christian teachers – integrating all of that. I'm still *transforming* if that's the right word. I'm much more secure in myself now than I ever was. And I'm still doing the work I need to do.

So many books have helped, I couldn't begin to name them – spiritual books, transformational books. I don't read much fictional material, but reading about who wrote the book gives it credence for me. What's their background, where are they coming from, what are their experiences? You know, there are so many people writing books whose history doesn't align. I just don't feel their depth. Someone takes a weekend workshop and all of a sudden they become experts.

As a metaphor for the process, I look at the seasons or the weather or the growing of a tree – how things happen with different environmental influences. How all the different influences affect things, and whether you do anything or not you're going to grow. We have seasons of our lives we can relate to the seasons of the year. There are times when you gather and grow, times when you have to give back. In the later years you're doing more service work, not struggling so much to survive or you get more security with yourself, whereas in the earlier years you're struggling to raise a family, slaying dragons. I think you gather and do a lot of work; then you need some time to digest it and to put it into practice. Then you go to another spurt, another *peduncle* as Chardin described it.

I'm 61 years old, definitely in my senior years, in the early winter of the process. I'm moving more and more into community work, more volunteer kinds of things, moving into that now in a conscious way and it feels good and feels right. Not that you can't do it in different part of your life. But I didn't do it earlier. I don't know if this is true of all Threes, but it might be that we do things alone and don't do a lot of things in groups. It's true for me that I've been pretty much of a loner. Not that I haven't worked with people, but I've been more self-sufficient. Now it's getting to be that I really enjoy sharing and working with others.

Chapter Three

Level by Level – Valerie's Story

I see transformation as growing, becoming healthier. One of my biggest growth periods came when I was diagnosed with a hole in my heart and had to have open-heart surgery. It was a totally new discovery. I was 31 years old when my OB detected a heart murmur and had me checked. That's how I found out.

The recovery period was painful and long because I had some complications and was sick for quite a while. Coming out of that experience got me to take a look at myself. At the same time I was in relationship with a guy I almost married, who broke off what I thought was an engagement. It wasn't formalized but we'd bought a ring. I was very emotionally vulnerable at that time, and he was a cardiologist, so he understood what was going on. It was really interesting because I was vulnerable and meek and during that time became much more submissive then I normally am. I sort of melted into his expectations and what he wanted, and was really not being myself. It wasn't until I began healing, physically and emotionally, that I started to experience the relationship and the surgery as a huge transformation.

This was a catalyst for me to really be thankful for what I have in my life, for my health, for my family, for the importance of friendships; to put things into perspective for what they really are, to not get so bent out of shape about insignificant things – getting upset because things weren't going right at work, with a boss, taking things personally, making big deals out of things like that. This experience got me to be more inner-directed, not caring so much what other people think. Also it was a catalyst to get me into a week-long *Life Success* seminar. That was a huge growing experience and this all took place within the timeframe of about a year.

Another big change for me was getting laid off from a prestigious, high-paying, fun sales job I'd had for four years. I'd been a very high producer, in the top 5% every year. I've always been a very high producer in every job I've had; always No. 1 or No. 2. So I was shocked, even though they laid off five positions like mine across the company. I had feelings of helplessness, of financial worry, and probably some ego associated with getting laid off – feeling out of control, insecure about the loss of the income, even though I had more money saved than I could ever need. And that's another good point. That whole transition helped me be not so financially concerned. I'm financially astute and still concerned about saving, and I manage all the finances and investments and bills, but that experience helped me let some of that go. You don't need as much money as you think you do to live.

That was very hard for me, but good in that it was also when my boyfriend and I became engaged. He moved here and I took the summer off. For three months I didn't work outside the home, which was a big growing process for me, letting go of that need to find a job again right away, to drive, drive, drive. I grew a beautiful vegetable garden in the back and it was great! I was tapping more into my creative side. In addition to the gardening I did some art work, painting, home-made gifts, making hand-painted napkins and things like that. That was really a good feeling for me because I do have that side, and when you're busying yourself with career, it's hard to find time for it. But it was a struggle for me, difficult to let go; I'd always been a hard-driving career person. And he was working in a new job, which brought up some issues for me in this new relationship, got me thinking about needing affirmation, of wanting him to come home at a reasonable hour because I was at home all day.

Having my son was a big change because it took away the need to task, task, task all the time. It seems I'm knocking that down a notch, level by level. Before I got married, I was very social, having people over for dinner, going out, doing things, traveling. And you can't do that very easily when you have a small child, without disrupting his schedule. It's interesting that it wasn't that difficult for me to slow my life down after him. I get pressure from friends who say, "I never see you anymore," and I've had to make a conscious effort to take a look at how many people I have in my life that I can really be close to and give time to. It felt kind of selfish in a way, to me, but I was very set that my family is my priority and my child is my priority. It's stressful sometimes, because I'm still filtering people out of my life. And you get pressure over that, someone calling and saying, "We never go out."

It's hard to set priorities sometimes, even with my closest friend. I spend more time with her than anyone else, but we don't spend nearly as much time together as we used to. It's been a transition for her, too, and we had to talk about it. But I feel strongly it was the right thing. It's taken my life down another notch. But still it's been a conscious effort. It hasn't been natural. I've had to think about my week and say to myself, *What am I going to do? No I'd better not do this. I've overextended my schedule and I'd better X that off my schedule.* I've had to do some work with it. Today I took my son in to the office while I was doing several errands, and I'm really in tune with *This is not good for him*. He's very happy at home where he can crawl around, go and take his nap. So I've started to say "No" more often. "No I can't come in for Friday morning meetings. I'll conference them if you want me to, but I'm not going to bring in my son, who's a toddler, when I'm supposed to have these days off." Before I would just do whatever was needed, what other people demanded.

There's been a transformation in my relationship with my husband in the last couple of months. I'm not sure what it all relates to, but we went through a rough period after the baby was born, as I guess most couples do. It shook up some things that we're both working on now. The main transformation from my perspective is that we're letting go of more issues, we're a little more careful of the battles we take on with each other, not taking on things that really don't matter so much.

For me the biggest change with my husband in the last two months has been that I'm trying to love and believe in who I am and what I am, and not take him so personally. I can give you a specific example, something that would have been a hot issue with me before. We went to a wedding, and someone said to me, "You've had a baby, and you look really good, like you've lost a lot of weight!" And he said, "Well, you don't know the whole story." I, of course, would have liked for him to say, "Doesn't she look great?" because I love those kind of compliments, especially from him in front of other people. That type of thing might have really, really gotten to me and I might have really gotten upset about it. It did jar me a little bit, but what I did instead was not put so much energy into it. I decided to have fun, have a nice evening. And I really did have a great time, with him!

It's been a couple of weeks, and I might bring it up to him, might say, "You know, I want to tell you something that happened at the wedding. I think at one point I might have made a big deal out of it, and I want you to know I didn't, but it did kind of bother me." I've been doing a lot less tamping down of my feelings. The way I'm articulating my feelings and holding my ground has been much less emotional, more courteous, whereas before it was more emotional, angry, accusatory and offensive. I think I'm becoming a lot better at giving it some time, not bursting out right away.

Sometimes it's enough to just stay with it, figure out what's going on with me. What's come to me in the last month or so is that it's better for me to say something if it's a really important issue. I'm doing it not so much to make a connection with him or get something from him, but because it's the right thing to do for me. It feels considerate of the other person, yet also saying something that's important to me. That I have a right to feel these things and I have a right to say them, and it's OK to say them, but let's say them in a way that's respectful. And that feels very good to me.

When people come at me in an aggressive way, if it's my husband or somebody at work, I still get defensive and my tendency is to want to come back in an aggressive way. I've gotten better at not lashing back so much, and I've tried to be aware that *OK, this person is aggressive and upset for a reason. There's something going on with them. It's not about me.* It happened this morning with my boss. I wanted her to look at a couple of things I'd brought in, and she was very short with me, probably more so than she's ever been. I took it a little bit personally, but I left her office and let it go. She did say, while I was on the way out, "I've got some real issues right now to deal with." I still want the business done, but I have to respect the fact that she has some issues to deal with.

I could go into this whole big deal like I might have done years ago, and say, "Put your issues aside! This is $200,000 worth of business we need to act on right now. I need the internal support to get this done! I brought in the business, I'm doing my job, it's your job to..." This would have been my old self talking. And it's still not easy for me because of my impatience. What's changed is that I don't act on it and I don't get so stressed out about it. I used to lose sleep over stuff like that, but I seldom lose sleep over my job anymore, which is huge for me.

After I was laid off, I worked for a year for a family-owned business that was completely horrible internally. It was not a good mix with me, having worked in big companies that had their issues, too, but they were at least fairly fine-tuned internally, they had goals. I could see the problems in this company as clear as day, and it was horrible. I was in sales and marketing and was supposed to bring in new clients, and I would just toss and turn and spend so much energy thinking, *How am I going to change this place? How am I going to bring in new clients and get more business when the internal structure is clearly not set up to handle it? All I'm going to be doing is bringing in new business and losing it*! It was clear to me what needed to be done, and I could get the top people in the company to admit to it, but they wouldn't execute. It was very frustrating. I spent time trying to fix it myself, much more outside my job description than I was supposed to be doing, and caring more about getting it done right than the owners!!!

And I was like that in all of my jobs, but that was the job where I started transforming into realizing, *It's just a job*! And something shifted permanently. I'm still conscientious about a lot of stuff, probably more than I should be, but there's a marked improvement. And I think that helped my husband, because he tends to get caught up with his job, too. He saw me when I was so stressed out all the time with my career and he saw the shift in me, which I think reminded him to try to do that.

It's helped a lot that I meet with a group of women regularly. We started when one of the women picked up a book called *Studying the Inner Child*, going back to your childhood, doing exercises, interviewing your parents, then sharing what you find with each other and telling how it relates to you today. After we finished that book, the group evolved into teaching each other things we think are important. The first one was the Enneagram. Then I had my neighbor who had breast cancer and a mastectomy come in and talk about what she had gone through and how she had been transformed because of this. Then one person suggested that everybody bring a book they're reading and highlight some of the key things they're learning. Occasionally we bring in a guest, someone we know who wants to experience what we're doing. In addition to our regular discussions, once a year we take a trip together, and we bring something to share. We have fun, too, and go hiking.

The Unity church helps, too. The lessons are really good, very applicable to everyday life. They have a saying each week and I have a couple of them on my refrigerator. They're into taking responsibility for your own life, not being victims. They have a guided meditation before the sermon or message for the day and it's a prelude to get you thinking. I try to do a little of that introspection every day, usually when my son is napping, to say, *Screw the house for a half hour, screw whatever else I have on my huge long list to do. I'm going to take this time right now, uninterrupted, and lie down for twenty minutes and just relax*. And I do a lot of reading. I'm reading a book called *In The Meantime* by a spiritual woman who's on Oprah a lot. I'm always reading one or two books at a time, and always with that flavor. I liked *The Celestine Prophecy*. I usually read at night for about twenty minutes before I go to sleep, or if I'm going somewhere on a plane. And then I've been reading a lot of kids' books, on the child's self-esteem and stuff like that.

My biggest resource has been my friendships with a few women who have a lot of depth, who are on the same track. We try to be very nonjudgmental with each other. We have fun, and we're very supportive of each other. I did stay involved with Life Success seminars for awhile. I haven't done as much of that lately but they have a celebration once a month after the seminar, and occasionally I'll go to those to bring back the whole experience, to get in touch with some of the pain I had in my childhood with my parents, to share that with people who care. Ultimately the *Life Success* seminar led to my forgiving my parents for some things I was holding onto. Taking responsibility for my own life was a key thing I learned, too. Stop blaming other people. I've also gotten myself to accept pain and not resist it so much. It seems like I spent a lot of my life resisting pain, but it's part of life and that's how I'm trying to look at it. I haven't been hit with a bomb yet, but I've been hit with some shrapnel from time to time. I'm trying to work with that, and it feels really good. Just being aware that pain is human, it's a normal part of life, it's OK and I'm going to live through it. And the *Life Success* seminar is where I met the women in my group.

I do a lot of seeking. I get information about seminars and one-day workshops. I don't go to all of them but I'm always interested in that sort of thing. Some I do with my husband, some with friends.

I think transformation has stages. I see it as level by level, taking things to the next level of growth. It seems that when you have some type of catastrophe or stress in your life, or a new variable, it jars new areas that you need to grow in. This never stops, and most of the time the levels go up, but sometimes you have to go through a valley to get up there. Overall, in my life there have been ups and downs but I keep going up. If I were to draw it, it would be somewhat like a funnel getting wider as it goes up.

It is so interesting to look at my boss, who's clearly a Three. She's thirty years old and does a fantastic job running the organization. She reminds me of how I was times ten, and that's phenomenal to me because I was extremely efficient. She can multi-task at such a high level of efficiency it just blows my mind, but she is so impatient with people. I know what that's like because I can get caught up into getting impatient with everything around me, other drivers, people at a store, people on the phone. I think that is a key problem with Threes. You have to get a grip on that because otherwise you're spinning your wheels your whole life, constantly being impatient with people, being stressed out because things aren't going as quickly as you want them to go, and probably not as quickly as you could make them go if the whole world was filled with people like you.

When I start getting that impatient feeling I try to realize, *Don't sweat this so much. Don't expect so much from people. Most people aren't going to be as results-oriented as you are. Most people aren't going to think about carrying everything up that's on the stairs when they go up, and putting it away like you do! And that's OK.*

Commentary

The overused gift of Style Three is to be outstanding. It is their Ego's way of drawing attention to itself. And theirs is a great gift: to be outstanding, successful and accomplished is to be really somebody! The two stories in this chapter illustrate what can happen when people move beyond the stories their Egos are telling. When they transform the need to be outstanding into something much more.

In these stories transformation "has stages [...], level by level, taking things to the next level of growth", as Valerie puts it. For Grant transformation involves a growing inner awareness. Each of these stages helps to relax Ego's control, so that more of the authentic can emerge in their lives.

A common trait of people of Style Three is to present an image that helps them appear to be outstanding in a given setting. This mask is part of Ego's story and becomes so important that they lose touch with themselves. In Grant's story, his key experience came when he hired a therapist to help him to sell real estate better. He found that to do that, he needed to learn about who he was so that he could connect more authentically with potential customers.

In moments when the Ego relaxes, people of Style Three can experience the virtue of *Truthfulness*, which Jerry Wagner describes as involving "being true to themselves. They realize they are who they are, and not the role they play, the social status they achieve, the works they perform, nor the tasks they accomplish." Grant likens this to the seasons of the year, there are times to gather and grow, times to give back. The acceptance of who and where he is plays a big part in being true to himself.

In Valerie's story, she experiences this truthfulness as the various levels that separate her from it are stripped away. Her story describes the key events in her life that have helped to weaken her Ego's armor of image, moments where she's in touch with her real self.

Her story provides several examples of how, when Ego is relaxed, a person of Style Three can experience the higher quality of *Hope* in the harmony of the universe. This hope supplies the antidote to the Ego-generated fear that they are not good enough, and will be seen to be not good enough. Valerie is valuable because she exists, not because of what she achieves, or what people think she has achieved. She is taking life down a notch, level by level. She is letting go of more issues. This, in turn, is allowing transformations in her most important relationships, with her son, her closest friend and her husband.

Today, Grant is more conscious of his image, which allows him to be more authentic. He illustrates by comparing how he was as a sports coach and how he is today as a minister. He has shifted from appearing good to being good. From being the person who needed to be out in front of the whole group to being someone who can be quietly inspirational.

The fixation is something that always remains, and the transformation process helps him to be more aware, more conscious, so that his behaviors and patterns change. Meditation helps him to see what is behind the image and be in touch with his internal processes.

Both describe in similar away how they get beyond the story their Ego is telling. As Grant puts it, "I'm still transforming, if that's the right word. I'm much more secure in myself now than I ever was. And I'm still doing the work I need to do." Valerie sees it "as level by level, taking things to the next level of growth. [...] This never stops, and most of the times the levels go up, but sometimes you have to go through a valley to get up there."

Three questions to ponder:

- How does the image I project keep my true self covered?

- What can I drop, in order to slow down?

- When did I last accept myself for what I am rather than what I have achieved?

Contents

1. Leaving the Drama Behind – Kathryn's story 55

2. The Richness of Being Real – Foster's Story 62

3. Commentary 70

Chapter Four – Style Four

Leaving the Drama Behind – Kathryn's story

The word *transformation* gives me a little bit of trouble because I tend to think of transforming *from* something *to* something, which is a one-shot deal, and that's not how I've experienced awakening in my life. Transformation is a word we use in the West because we want to get someplace. I think of an evolution of consciousness that's endless, and in the process of our evolution we have things that block us. Leonard Laskow speaks of *treasured wounds*. So for me the exploration is seeing how I've held things that kept me from moving forward.

My process of evolution probably started when I was in college. That's when I became clinically depressed. I've been searching my whole life, but it was more critical then. In graduate school I got to where I couldn't move off my couch, and finally dragged myself to a walk-in clinic and saw a therapist. I started to confront some childhood relationships, and realized my whole life I'd hit walls where I couldn't contain the emotions; unfortunately more times than I care to quote.

The first thread in the process has been putting myself in situations that pushed the envelope for me – because I valued work and I'd put myself with people who pushed me, personally and professionally. The other thread is more therapeutic, trying to figure out why the pain was there, why the depression was there, *Why is this so hard*? And I think both helped me evolve my consciousness; all are pieces of the total. I have a DNA image of two strands interwoven but moving towards a destination.

The other image I have is two ends of a continuum: along the way you either move from pain or you move toward possibilities. As you resolve more and more of the pain issues, you move toward the possibilities, toward what you want to create at the other end. I started with more pain in my life and right now it's a mixture of both. Moments closer to the possibility end have often been from intellectual stimulation. An example is a professor who took me under his wing when I was an undergraduate. I became involved in his experiments and loved doing it, but working with him also pushed me into taking responsibility for areas I didn't know much about. It was the same thing in graduate school. I hated school so I applied for a fellowship to help teach the Psychology of Interpersonal Relationships course. I walked in and the professor said, "Sure, you can be on staff." And I thought, *Who, me?* I couldn't believe it. I learned a lot and was always on the edge of what I thought I knew how to do.

Many of my stories are about people who saw potential in me I didn't see in myself. If they hadn't pushed I wouldn't have grabbed them by the neck and said, "I want to do this!" Later on, when I was working in a large corporation, I again attached myself to someone who always pushed me. I loved his clarity of language. I remember a situation where he told me, "You've got to go over that person's head," and I said, "You can't do that." Essentially he pushed me to "do what you believe in," to be more than I was at the moment. I've always been attracted to those kinds of relationships.

Sometimes I'm embarrassed. If you knew the number of times I went for help… like other people don't do that. Now the painful end doesn't hit me so severely. I feel I understand many of the core issues and it doesn't have the same hold it used to have on me. I get bouts of depression, but I haven't been clinically depressed in a long time.

One of my core issues is feeling I'm not good enough, and this has come out in a number of different ways. Another issue is denying myself, either in wanting others' approval or in taking on the energy of other people in a way that affects my own. Early on I had so little sense of myself; I gave so much of myself away. At some level in my mind I didn't exist. And actually one of my main coping mechanisms was to go away: I used to go away in my head a lot. I finally figured out if there was reincarnation I'd just have to come back. So, many of my struggles have been in learning to get past the going away, to stay in real time, in the midst of whatever was scaring me, which was usually some threat, and often the threat was around not knowing.

I was always rewarded for what I did, so I put a lot of energy into being right. It was like being a One, but not a One; it was a strategy for me. And the more you do that, the more dysfunctional you get. Part of the pattern is proving to yourself there's something terribly wrong with you. Once, when things weren't going well, I started having tunnel vision. I was self-aware enough to stop and breathe and shift. But it took many of those experiences, of not knowing what was going on, to stop feeling like a failure. I did a lot of work on *It's OK not to know, I really am OK.*

And there's so much out there like the Enneagram – if you want help, it's out there, from body work to energetic work; you name it. I think you start with where your interests are. When people follow what they're attracted to, that's the grand scheme. There really is a grand scheme and there's no manual – it comes a paragraph at a time, and it's not necessarily through therapy. It's what your heart is calling you to do; and there's usually a gift in it, an experience you need so you can become fuller. Sometimes I've actively sought therapy, saying to myself, *I need help; I can't get through this. I need structure and someplace to do that.* I got really good at using therapy for specific issues, and milked it for what it was worth. With some therapists, I just needed to stay out of my way while I did what I needed to do.

Yoga classes helped me in ways I didn't understand at the time. In graduate school I'd be so outside myself, I'd walk into doorjambs. Yoga helped me get in touch with my body. And dance helped me – I never formally danced, but I was really attracted to it. Most people go to discos to pick people up. I went to dance.

There were many times when people just cared. When you're coming from that place of feeling like shit, it's grace to have people who care, and I've been blessed with a lot of grace in my life.

I also started thinking about alternative religious approaches. As a kid I always had a strong religious connection but the church wasn't doing it for me. I read *The Autobiography of a Yoga* and started working with some of those teachings and meditation practices. I've had moments that were such gifts. When my job took me to the West Coast I drove up to a lake by a temple of the Self-Realization Fellowship, based on the teachings of Yogananda, and went to a service. This was another one of those times when I was feeling not good, and it was so clear that I got a shot of love. It lasted only about five seconds – I couldn't hold it – but I never forgot it. A Yogananda disciple has a retreat center in northern Michigan, The Ranch, and I always get help when I go there. Once when my husband and I were having a hard time, Yogananda's disciple came to me in my sleep and helped me. If you take a step, the universe really does answer. When you send out intent, you send out vibrations. If you put out effort, you get three times the help back.

There have been times when I had clear choices as to whether I was going to go on or not. Not that I was suicidal, but I thought I'd go crazy. There were times when I'd lie in bed and feel there was a battle between light and darkness inside, and consciously choose God and light. The first few years of my marriage were so hard, and any number of times I felt like walking. But I knew I needed to stay with it, to learn to love, even though it made no sense – there were problems that were way over my head. And I'm glad I stayed with it; I've learned a lot.

But those situations felt more traumatic than transformational. They're more dramatic but I'm not sure making a different choice would have been any more lethal. For example, if I'd stayed in my corporate job instead of leaving, maybe I would have lost my soul. The more dramatic stuff is more visible, but the slow death can be more insidious. Maybe the more dramatic stuff forces us to notice.

The earlier problem was allowing myself to be talked out of my view of reality. Often my husband's reaction was "You're making this a problem; our situation is not that bad." We went into therapy at the time, but he dropped out – though toward the end he began to work on himself. What changed in me was not blaming myself as much. And now I think we're really good at pulling back and each working on our own pieces. I've gotten better at saying, *This is my reality and it may not be right, but I'm going to hang in there with it*. During the transition phase I was hardening myself to hold my position. Now I can do it more gently. I went from *It's all my problem*, to *It's not at all my problem* and digging in, to now becoming an observer of all that.

There's a process of change for all of us from (1) you're in it but you don't know you're in it, to (2) you know you're in it but you don't know what to do about it, to (3) you know you're in it and you know what to do about it.

I've gotten in my own way at times by deflecting input. *I try so hard, how can that be happening*? Because it was all or nothing in my head: *If I admit I was wrong I would be really flawed*. So somehow, trying so hard was "enough." It took me a long time to even understand what I was doing there. Always wanting to do it my own way, believing I was somehow above the rules and regulations, was a more subtle way of resisting insight. I don't mean following your heart, I mean obstinately.

To keep myself conscious I do structured meditation at least once a day – and it ought to be twice a day, but I have a hard time with that second meditation. It's really being with myself, having a structure in place that reinforces those things I'm learning. That's why I go to The Ranch. It's a course correction, to stay conscious. I have a New Year's Reflection Day. And I still journal a lot – that word means different things to different people. If something's bothering me I draw a line down the middle of the page. On one side is Self; on the other side is anything from a body part to an emotion to an event – and I talk to it. Or I use mind mapping to help me understand things. The issue goes in the center with everything connected to it radiating out from the center. I allow myself to stay with what's bothering me.

It also helps to keep energy moving when I'm under a lot of pressure – yoga, dance, massages. When I was doing a lot of therapy I had a massage at least once a week. The Pilates work I'm doing now helps. I've always read a lot. I think sometimes I read because I need to understand on an intellectual level, but if I stop there it doesn't go anywhere. I have to take it to a deeper level. I try to read something inspirational every night before I go to bed; I think what you put in your head the last thing at night is important.

When I had breast cancer several years ago, I learned to go inside, listen, and trust myself. No matter how it came out, I felt compelled to listen to myself and to work holistically with the cancer, going to therapy, creating emotional support in my life. It wasn't until three years later that an image came up out of that breast that made me realize there were still unfinished issues with my Mom – how I take on some other peoples' stuff.

I'm happier now than I've ever been before. I'm lighter, more present, so things are getting better. If someone asks, "Why go through stuff?" I'd say, "Because it gets better." Even though there's a lot happening now in my life, it's comparatively OK. I still get caught, but I get uncaught more quickly. In Enneagram terms, *Serenity* or *Equanimity* is supposed to be my virtue. I wrote an article about how my ongoing lesson has been to leave the drama behind:

> Recently a friend and teacher suggested I was too caught up in the drama of a family situation. My involuntary reaction was to guffaw. I mean, how could she be so sure? Besides, I was clear I'd worked hard to stay out of the drama and thought I was doing quite well. However, her comment kept running through my mind. What drama could she be referring to?
>
> I've known for some time it's been a challenge for me to be happy when others around me are not. Also, I've seen how feeling responsible for others drives me to try to make things *better* even if it means fixing their lives. But through the years I've made considerable progress in both these areas. I no

longer think I can control another person, solve their problems or make them happy. I have come to humbly acknowledge I don't even know what's best for them. So I was surprised by the suggestion that I was hooked into the drama of the situation.

But I knew better than to ignore my friend's observation. I started listening to myself with a new consciousness. I was amazed at how often I would respond to "How are you?" with a litany of what was going on in the lives of those around me. Was I really using others' dramas to define my own life? It seemed ridiculous. Yet, I began to see that focusing on others used up time and energy I needed to focus on my own life. It was a diversion that let me off the hook. Who would blame me for not doing more when my plate was full? Clearly, this pattern was not serving me well.

Then I started listening to how I talked about my own life. That, too, had a dramatic flair. Where did I learn that everything had to be *bigger than life, full of problems to overcome, mountains to climb*? (Drama, by the way, seems to need a bit of gloom and doom and danger to give it juice.)

This new awareness comes in the middle of a journey I started six months ago. As an experiment, I committed to listening for inner direction as opposed to reactively doing things to fill up time or to get work. Well, I have been listening but the messages haven't been what I expected. The messages have been to *Let go of things (simplify possessions), do less (simplify life), go inside (stop relying on outside information and expertise)*. So I've been throwing things out, canceling subscriptions, pulling back from professional meetings, and generally spending more time with myself.

As I think about it, there's a clear connection between *being hooked on drama* and the journey I'm on. Drama was and is another diversion. Drama is a way for me to feel important, to fill time with "meaningful" activity. I could sense a panic deep inside as I considered giving up the melodrama. All this pulling back was creating a huge void. Without drama I'd feel naked and vulnerable. No excuses, nothing to make me special. It was scary.

There are a number of lessons for me here. One is to trust that what and where I am right now, without any exaggeration or drama, is enough. Another is that life without drama isn't mediocre or bland; it's living from the center. The events or people in my life weren't the problem, it was the emotional energy I gave to them – I would lose my sense of self, and stop listening to my inner guidance.

Drama pulled me away from my heart. Today is a good day to let go of the baggage getting in the way of my being in my heart. For this, I will gladly leave the drama behind.

The Richness of Being Real – Foster's Story

In a Twelve Step conversation parallel to the idea of *transformation*, there are people who insist they have *recovered* and others who say – with equal vehemence – "No, I'm *recovering*." For example, to speak of the Four's shame thing as having been transformed and to speak eloquently as to how that has occurred makes me laugh. Rather, isn't our task one of *transforming*? You know, keep it present tense. And maybe both meanings of the word *tense* apply! It is present tense and it's still *dynamic*, it could still go either way. We're surprised when *Suddenly I'm back, smack-dab in the center of my pattern again*? It's a tough sell, though. It's a hell of a lot easier to sell the bright-penny solution. People don't want neutrality or an invitation to more vigilance. How exhausting!

It might be my Four bias that's leading toward the idea that the best we can get is not some orgasmic enlightenment bullshit; but really what we get is *neutrality*. That's what *presence* is: *I'm not putting anything in and I'm not grabbing anything out. It's just here*. It's the neutrality of presence that fits with the notion of *equanimity*.

There's a possible framing, though, that doesn't have to look totally desirable, but it's a reality, and valuable without being orgasmic. From a coaching perspective, that's the solidity you want to offer to people, that it's possible and it doesn't have to be all wrapped up in the ego package. It might also be approached with some reverence.

Part of my struggle as a Four is that *introjection* is pretty central, and still bites me in the ass. For example, my *idealized picture* of someone I just talked with was suddenly jarred by what was *actually* happening. And, truthfully, his loving friendship with me is still in what occurred. It's just not happening the way I think it should. It's that introject/controlling piece. And, *When will this stop biting me in the ass*? The *surprise* of it, when it occurs to me, *My God, I'm in a confused and suffering and ungrounded state right now*, this point where finding ground is more difficult for me.

I'd like to think I've made more progress, but when the opposite is happening, it's played as panic: *Oh my God, this isn't what I thought it was*. Right next to that is the *shame* piece, *How humiliating that I had this wrong*. And with it comes blame, *How dare he do this*? I don't know what you'd name that; maybe "The Flat-Out Emotional Wad."

What does anybody do when they don't get what they want? They're suffering their hit, their discomfort. I don't know why Fours' pain would be any different than anybody else's pain. But that's not going to stop me from spinning my imagination about it, either. Maybe it's about the *crash* out of the satisfying fantasy – it's expressed through some sort of exaggeration, just like the fantasy was. Maybe the key word is *want*. What can I accept in a real way? Because I'm more comfortable with the grand extremities and maybe that's why I have Nines who are buddies: the calmer, loving center is the part I don't particularly gravitate toward. Nines feel the need to go farther out and Fours are saying, *Oh, getting closer to the center is so much more restful*.

You could evoke the idea of *Equanimity*, that there might be some balance between either grand success or hideous failure, that there might be some grey area that includes both. The tripping point of *envy* is giving it *so* much importance that it would go one way or the other. Releasing that means the cue here is not necessarily to avoid the pain of something but to avoid the extremity of feeling. And that includes feeling good. How much does *that* suck? I *have to watch when I'm feeling good, because it's slippery*!

The break on the introject situation this morning, interestingly enough, was centered on the idea that he and I were not on the same page. An engaging conversation that's mutually beneficial is a little bit of heaven. In this situation I was being called out for detracting from this, as if it were all my fault, which made me angry. Part of that, too, was feeling a lack of mutuality. In the olden days, in the Myers-Briggs days, I was bemoaning the liabilities in my being such an "N" and such a "P." The bottom line was feeling victimized by "J." *You know, I bring something here with what I do*! I remember exactly where I was standing when this occurred. I sort of put a stake in the ground: *What I bring has value and I will put it at the center of the table*. Somehow or other my willingness to do that was part of that manifesto. And my criticism of the "J" person with whom I was locking horns was that in some ways my ability to go to the center of the table might not be about "P" or "N" or anything else; stepping to the middle of the table became very, very important to me.

In the situation I'm still processing from today, it seems the other person didn't step to the middle. There was a *betrayal of the middle*, which is something I can do, or the other person can do. Interestingly enough, what he was calling me on was that I was *not* staying present, that I was expressing something by running through my pattern. I didn't feel that was as true as he was making it out to be. This speaks to equanimity – that middle ground.

For many years the idea was to somehow watch *envy* accelerate, which was around comparative thinking. It's interesting that I have a fresh example of the introject tripping me up, because when you asked for an example from the past, I thought of a situation where I realized the key player in my accelerating envy was actually the introject. That story is about private time together with an old friend: She and I were one-on-one, both one-half of couples, settling in, having a conversation, and this was like a great big, triple-chocolate sundae for me, a connection party where there would be some depth. So it was a slippery slope to start with and I was marginally aware of that and, of course, my expectations were running high.

In the course of that conversation I was doing an update about something going on in my life, and hell, damn, and tarnation, she responded by taking the side of the person I was telling the story about. At which point it was *Color me surprised*, jaw dropped, astonishment, *How could this possibly be*? Hurt, wounded, abandoned; all those juicy things. I got through the rest of that visit, then left and was running the whole thing, ramping up the emotions, knowing that was crazy, knowing the humiliation factor, too. Her taking this other person's side made me the *less than*. I was processing all of this and in my cups with it, and I don't know where exactly it came from, but the *introject* notion came along; a reality check – the most painful thing for a Four. But I managed to get to: *Wait a minute! This friend of mine is acting the way she has always acted. Her defense of this other person fits into many of her patterns. The fact that she would call me out on this re: her truth is very much the person I've always known. So what's different about this particular situation, to have me in the state I'm in? It's the introject. I'm wanting her to be different than she is.*

It's so simple, but I had completely bought my own version of the story. Creating it yourself goes to some of the Almaas stuff. This ego didn't come from nowhere. There was a conversation this morning around the ability to talk about something like "organizational soul."

Chapter Four

And I thought, *Well, wait a minute, that's what the Enneagram language is for us.* We can actually get to the point where I'm able to say something about my soul is predicated on a value system of personal connection; indivisible, personal connection. So what do I do? I create a little package for myself and I'm severely thrown on my pins when it's challenged. We designed the introjection tool and then we figured out when to use it. It's more difficult to see the *pattern* than to see the historical event. But trust me, it's part of the pattern!

I will tell the story of another weaving of introject. The big tripping point word for Fours, I think, is *real*. If there is a panic point for me, when I'm tripping over into a big crash, the core panic is that *I'm not real. I'm nothing. I'm not real* is a very subtle and seductive black hole to fall into. So in this other story I was probably in my forties, and my mother and I were having a conversation. Somehow it queued up that Mom talked about a time she remembered when I was little, that I looked up at her and she would never forget how much I loved her, the way I was looking at her. She was so happy to say that. It was an *event* for her. I'm the fifth of seven children, so you can imagine how worn out my mother was! Her saying that really moved me. And that she had any memory of me at all! There's a hit in that of, *Oh my gosh, my reality was there and taken in.*

"To be taken in" would be the phrase. See how that might be a slip of the introject? I must take it in because nobody's about to take *me* in. The symmetry of that is part of the story. What Mom didn't know when she was telling me about her memory was that it corroborated a memory of my own, which is a screaming Four story. I know it was after we moved, so I was maybe a year and a half, two years old. And my mother had these younger kids around; one of the older ones was a toddler, I guess. At a time when I was having my diapers changed there was a commotion outside the door and Mom left.

This is an aside – the screaming in that house wasn't like a horror movie, but it was my mother's hyperactive Six terror button.

Here's this classic early abandonment thing. I was high and dry on this bassinette, big-time exposed; I couldn't get down from there, couldn't even sit up. Flat-out terrified, I just lay there. And Mom, bless her heart, was fumbling around doing something and all of a sudden remembered she'd left me there. She didn't scream again, but I felt all her guilt, all this upset, so when she got back to the bassinette I have it made up in my mind *that's* when I looked at her the way she remembers me looking at her. And that was the introject – it's in the books: *I can't depend on you. The only way I'm going to have my piece of you is if I take you inside.* And she saw it happen.

I'm much more real than I imagine myself to be. In fact, I don't have to imagine myself be anything at all. I already am. I'm present in my own story. The pattern kicks in when I start to embellish – and that's what my friend was calling me on this morning, the amount of embellishment I was adding to stories. And that's valid and fair. Like we all do, I'm going to pick up my pattern, play with my ego tools, and for the Four it's to prove that I exist. And the embellishment is around the belief that there *isn't* a story, that there might not be a story.

That's the *real/unreal* tension – the belief that "more story" can compensate for the fact that there's *no* story. And the delusion is that there's no story. There's a story – it happens to be solo on the bassinette! I can forgive somebody for making some shit up if the story doesn't work for them.

The memory I had was the *abandonment* part of it. I'm only *imagining* the introject part. I know my mother returned. And it's interesting where the selective memory is – I can remember her consternation at having left me there. So that was proof that my mother loved me. I don't think I read that on her face. That's not part of my memory. Only that I was relieved she was there. I remember the *feeling* of abandonment and the *feeling* of relief, which signals something else. Feeling was all I had. And, going back to how we opened this, it's a lifetime gift! The gift that keeps on giving!

Earlier in my life, as I went through my forms of self-abuse, which for me was to flail and flog my emotions into some form of identity I was not particularly kind to myself. Drama language! But that's what it felt like. And that's still a struggle. I still need help from around me to notice I'm hurting myself. It's a strange little corner. And it's usually the same thing; it's around ramping up emotions, that somehow or another I will be more real if I am feeling this intensely. A character on a TV show years ago described himself as "an emotional cutter." I laugh, but there's a reality to that very Four image; the cry for attention, heightening some experience to the point where it's got to be visible. It must be specific in order to create a worthy identity of some kind, and it temporarily relieves the Four anxiety that *I'm not real.*

I asked an Eight wife what it was like to fight with her Four husband. She beautifully said, "Well, as you'd expect I fight with my fists." "And what about him, the Four?" She smiled and said, "Razor blades." So if you're going to hurt somebody, you know where they hurt. And you turn that on yourself. The precision of suffering, pain for a purpose takes *years* of practice! What's different today is that I'm not the pain broker I used to be. I'd like to think I've established some other forms of currency that will make me feel much richer. There's affection, there's truth. I'm starting to feel there's hearts and flowers around it. How *common* and *less than*!

Levels of dialogue will help me calm anxiety and be as real as I can be. In the Twelve Step program I'm a part of, co-dependence has to be addressed. That comes back around to dealing with one's own reality. Other things that help, and it's related to that, are around community involvement. I was part of theater endeavors for years. Those were also circles of people with common interests. I've found that some groundedness in like-minded folk keeps my Four from running loose in the street. In the men's spirituality groups I've been in for my later-life growth, we not only have common interests but common identity. A way to explore the different facets of my own identify has been very reassuring. I'm so convinced I'm not real and with that, not worthy and all the other Four stuff, that to be among people who are tribal connections reassures my own reality.

Also what pops to mind is not something you *do* but something you *get*. I can remember, when my partner was dying in the eighties, thinking, *No one can take this experience away from me.* To somehow claim something as *mine* weaves in with the grounded sense of my own reality. I don't think I could ever advise a Four to go out and look for an experience like that, but to be open to it when it arrives and to recognize this is a confirmation of your own substance, your own reality, and nobody is going to take that away from you. Nobody can.

This is relevant because I've come up with ideas and later heard someone else espouse the same idea and forget they heard it from me. Or even, and this is difficult for me to this day, to see how one of my ideas has circled around and come through somebody else could almost be construed as validating. *That's my idea! I know that's my idea.* Having some friends to parse that with is helpful, but nobody has taken it away from you if it's your idea. Even as I say that, I don't really believe myself. *How dare they? Don't they know?*

Good friends help me claim my experience. And I *am* somebody. I don't have to be spinning a wild tale or emotionally cutting to have my story told and heard. And the fact that I'm real is a better story. And there's the joke. Maybe there's another metaphor in this. It's like the freak show, we're all in little booths along the midway. Or after death we go backstage and I get to tell my father, "You know, your portrayal of a right-wing capitalist pig was brilliant! *Very* convincing!"

Journaling is huge for me. The joke line with journaling is *How can I expect anybody else to listen to me if I don't listen to myself?* There's a lot of whining in my journals, and there's poetry that comes out of better sessions, for which I'm very grateful. On the poetry side, I've noticed over the years that journaling helps me enter linear time. That may sound preposterous or pretentious, but there's a felt reality there. In some ways it comes down to being *here*, on this planet. I resist that and journaling helps me step it down. The panic that I'm not real… write it out, write it out. You know how a cat goes up the drapes? Getting myself *down off the drapes* is part of what the journaling experience involves for me. Sometimes my partner will tell me I've lapsed in my journaling and I need to get back to it, which means I'm walking around a little bit crazy and ungrounded and *up the drapes.*

The other practice, for all this resistance to my own reality, is yoga. I don't keep it alive or as disciplined as I once did, but to become more present to my physical being, to experience alignment, has been of great service.

With that, too, are images on sailboats years ago. Being in the sailing world was how I managed to survive my teenage years, When you think about sailing, it's creating some balance in the center of a lot of chaos. That was a physical reality for me – saved my sanity in a lot of ways, to have an experience of stillness and order and I could be at the center of that, was a *huge* relief from the turmoil I was experiencing in just about everything else.

You could also talk about theater doing the same thing. Theater fed a lot of things – communal learning, shared values, where a relationship with fantasy was allowed and I could explore who I was. And, also true of a lot of group environments, to see people who were a bigger mess than I could ever hope to be.

I'm thinking of some uggabugga Enneagram person years ago talking about the direction of energy and I kind of stepped into a big *downward* thrust for Fours. You know, reality means *I'm here now* and the notion of *into the earth* in where I am right now. When I think about *down*, there's also an idea of *spreading*. The bigness that appeals to me is not in the air but in the earth. It's also *substance*. Air is ethereal, up, other. Here, now, and the richness of being as real as this, down into the earth, has some notion of transformative energy for me. It's about being more fully a part of physical existence.

I would also speak to something transforming in laughter. A butchered paraphrase of the Buddhist sage would be: "Silliness is being in the presence of something that is just outside our understanding." I take that to be something about the giddiness of laughter. And maybe laughter is a signal, as well, that in my big attachment to nothing and what's missing as something to agonize over, what's more fun than being tickled by something new? I am welcoming it and it is welcoming me. And that, for me, is in laughing with friends. Not being stupid and gloomy, but on that edge of letting reality grow.

Commentary

The overused gift of Style Four is to be unique. It is their Ego's way of attracting attention. This is a great gift, for who can be unique is really somebody, definitely not a Joe or Josephine Average. The two stories in this chapter illustrate what can happen when people of Style Four move beyond the story their Egos are telling. When they transform the need to be unique into something much, much more.

In these stories, both Kathryn and Foster prefer to think in terms of *transforming* rather than transformation, "an evolution of consciousness that's endless," as Kathryn describes it. She continues, "For me the exploration is seeing how I've held things that kept me from moving forward." Foster says, "You know, keep it present tense. And maybe both meanings of the word *tense* apply!" Their comments illustrate how keeping it present helps to relax Ego's control, so they connect naturally to the world.

A sense of inadequacy, of not being enough, is a common trait of people of Style Four. Foster's story shows one form of this when he describes in exquisite detail his inner response to an encounter with a friend just before his interview for this book. It first took the form of panic because his idealized view of the relationship jarred with reality. This quickly turned to shame: "How humiliating that I had this wrong."

In moments when Ego relaxes, a person of Style Four can experience the virtue of *Equanimity*, described by Jerry Wagner as realizing "the beloved they have been so searching for outside themselves dwells within them, when they realize that they are naturally connected to and are at home in themselves and the world."

In Kathryn's story, this takes the form of leaving behind the drama, letting go of the baggage that pulls her away from her heart. As she listens for inner direction she receives messages to support this: "*Let go of things (simplify possessions), do less (simplify life), go inside (stop relying on outside information and expertise).*"

Foster describes his Ego armor in terms of dramatic experiences, his tendency to embellish events so they either illustrate grand success or hideous failure. His story charts the moments that helped him find a balance point between these extremes, a grey area that includes both. Of course, this also means he has to be careful when he's feeling good, as this can easily lead to an extreme. In moments when Ego is relaxed, he experiences the higher quality of *Originality*, he realizes he is connected with those around him and the cosmos itself, and there is no need to re-establish this connection.

Today, Foster describes his experience of presence as "*I'm not putting anything in and I'm not grabbing anything out. It's just here.* It's the neutrality of presence that fits with the notion of equanimity." He's found that groundedness with like-minded folks helps him claim this experience. He realizes he doesn't need to be spinning a wild tale in order to have his story heard.

Kathryn is happier now than she's ever been. She's lighter and more present, signs for her that things are getting better. Processing what comes up helps her leave the drama behind: to let go of things, do less and go inside. As she puts it: "Drama pulled me away from my heart. Today is a good day to let go of the baggage getting in the way of being in my heart. For this, I will gladly leave the drama behind."

Three questions to ponder:

- In what ways does drama distract me from my heart?

- How often do I take time to notice what's happening now?

- How do I recognize my equanimity?

Contents

1. Out of the Biosphere – Peter's story	73
2. The Hero's Story – David's Story	77
3. Commentary	81

Chapter Five – Style Five

Out of the Biosphere – Peter's story

To me, *transformation* is similar to the notion of conversion – coming in possession of a quality that's a gift, that's beyond your own making. My big change happened at age thirty in a *Cursillo* group, a short course in Christianity; not as in *academic course* but as in *a journey together*. I was kind of conned into going because my wife wanted to go and this was the seventies where, if you were married, your husband had to precede you through the course. I'd come to a place in life where God was a stern taskmaster and I started out thinking *OK, I'm just here, checking off the box so my wife can come.* I think it was the intensity of the experience that allowed me to come into that relationship with God, because somewhere, through all the intensity, my resistance and mind-set let go. The authenticity of who these people were got through to me; just lay people giving witness from their own experience. The character of what they said was very real, and I couldn't attribute it to canned or pious ritual. What spoke to me was how they had changed. Richard Rohr says, "The power is in the person," and that's what touched me.

As a result of my *Cursillo* experience, I've never been the same. Initially, however, it had a major disorienting effect. It was awful! On my first day back to work after that weekend I left early. I'm an engineer, and prior to that weekend my attitude toward people who worked in the plant was, *They're just dummies, and you have to placate them in whatever way necessary to get them to do what they should do by themselves.* As a Five I was using rigid compartmentalization, thinking these people had a mission to do as little possible and get as much money and bennies as they could. It was kind of degrading, but it had worked for me in the past. However, after that weekend I had no way to relate. I thought, *This doesn't work, I can't function.* And I left with such a horrible headache. It was like being put in a different land where the language isn't the same anymore. It took a while to re-orient, but I began to see those people as children of God instead of dumb-ass union guys who didn't want to work. And the shift in my thinking was a one-way thing. Having gone there, I couldn't go back.

Ten years later, again because my wife had an interest, I went through a program in charismatic prayer reading. What had bothered me most about the charismatic people was this "Jesus told me" stuff, assuming they had a direct channel and there were no gray areas. In my old, lofty Five mind-set, I thought of these people as kind of goofy. There were some who were just adopting clichés, but as I hung around them over time I began to see that others were being genuine. Over a period of three to four years I felt an excitement that scripture readings had as much to do with current times as when they were written, and they brought me both peace and challenge.

I've also had creative insights on my job that are quantum shifts in doing something I would never have done. I'll work hard trying to come up with some approach to a concept, pursuing every possible avenue until I'm exhausted, tell myself, *It's just not there, it's just not doable*, and then Bingo!!! At first I don't trust it; I have to sit with it a while. I had one experience where, after several weeks and exhausting the experts, I got a dramatic idea that I knew instantly would work. But I didn't tell anybody where I got the idea because several people commented that it was kind of a bizarre solution. After a year there weren't any problems, and I'd been thinking for a long time, *I need to share this*, so when it came up again in a meeting I felt compelled to say the idea came from "Divine insight, a gift from God." This was kind of like farting in church – nobody said a word!

In addition to the *Cursillo* group I've put a lot of emphasis on meditation, on contemplation – suspending things and trying to be in touch with the body, experiencing the action of the gut and the breath. I struggle, wondering *What does that really mean and do I even really feel it?* But I've experienced enough to give me hope for that kind of union.

The Enneagram is useful preparation for transforming because it helps me perceive and understand myself and my life as it is. When I first started getting more serious with the Enneagram, I listened to Helen Palmer's meditation tapes that focus on breathing and suspending your thinking. That for me was like when I was learning how to swim. Oh, it was terrifying! *If I stop thinking I don't know if I will exist; it will be like going under water.* Daily I would reach that point where I'd think less and less and then get too scared and stop. It was very slow, like going into a swimming pool, knowing the water's cold, and dipping your toes first, and then your ankles, and then up to your knees. I finally got to the place where I wasn't thinking at all, and that was a real place of freedom – I could exist without thinking. For me it's important to have a discipline to shut off my damned mind. It may be only for seconds. But if I can do that, then I can shut it off at other times, too.

The ongoing challenge of being a Five is a view that life is a Zero Sum Game – there are only so many resources, so you have to hold on to what you have. The daily effort for me is seeing that distortion, going against the bias to withdraw because I'm thinking *I'm going to lose something here*. The piece that's trying to get through to me now is recognizing how much I want to be in control, to create a secure environment. For example, in staff meetings I'm biased to sit there and try to analyze what's going on rather than engage. Maybe I'll ask a kind of passive-aggressive question, like throwing a rock. Or I'll ask an open-ended question as a feeler, a question so ambiguous it's not clear to anyone but me, and then pull back to see if people are going to pounce on me. If I do that, I can leave feeling bitter, and think, *What a bunch of yo-yos – they're only concerned about their political interests and don't give a rat's ass about anything*! I can be a participant in the group when I raise a question with a lead-in about why it's relevant – either its consequences or its benefits – in such a way that I'm in the conversation.

But I get in my own way with the bias to withdraw into my little biosphere. There are moments of grace when I'm aware this bias is in process and, if I choose to call it, I have the potential for being a whole lot different. When I've done that and stayed with it, I've gotten myself out of a container and been a contributor and a participant with other people. Otherwise I just stay in my little biosphere.

I ask myself, Could *there really be a life outside the biosphere*? At times I think I've just scratched the surface. For me the most recent example of being stuck in the resistance stage of change is thinking, *I'm not sure I've ever had a genuine feeling. Maybe I've only had thoughts about feelings*. That depressed me for a long time. So I can't always cycle through.

Sometimes I can put myself in a place where it's possible for grace to break through, by just getting out of the way, by not cooperating with the compulsive energy. At those times I can recognize what I'm doing – I don't know if it's conscience or what Palmer calls *the inner observer* – that faculty can tell me my mind is running, it's in control.

When it's the inner observer and not the ego operating, I feel an at-easeness, a relaxation where my body's not on edge. The best indicator for me is that I'm not attached to the outcome. Whatever happens is OK. It's not a mental construct, but rather a receptive state: less guarded, and feeling *I'm here.*

Chapter Five

The Hero's Journey – David's Story

To me, transformation is moving from one consistent and orderly psychic state to another more consistent and more integrated psychic state. The Enneagram provides a context to become aware of the assumptions, biases, and limitations of my point group and begin consciously choosing different assumptions and points of view.

I can think of many times when I had flashes of insight where I've seen things in a different way than I'd ever expected. I changed in college – just from attending classes and having conversations with fellow students. In a Freshman philosophy class we discussed how God could not contradict Himself. And I said to the professor in this very naïve voice, "You mean, God cannot do everything?" That was a flash of insight for me.

An interest in Jung came from my mid-life issues: I saw the Jungian approach as a way to understand men and women and their roles. My Myers-Briggs interest came from job-related needs to help people understand themselves in a career context; however, the depth of interest came in realizing this approach was a fascinating way to understand myself and others. My attraction to the Enneagram came from curiosity: *Is this a real system? Why are so many people fascinated by it?* I'm still trying to understand why I got this direction. Part of it came from hearing about transformation in an Enneagram context, particularly what Helen Palmer had to say about developing the inner observer. Part of it came from a retreat experience where we practiced meditation, and from a meditation group I later joined.

I've also had an experience of dramatic emotional change. I did everything in the world to keep my first marriage from ending, and when it finally did happen it was a blow to my self-esteem. Specifically, I realized I didn't really understand what feelings were all about. My wife would accuse me of not having feelings, of being too logical, and I didn't know what she was talking about.

Finally, I realized intellectually I needed to do something, and that's when I got involved in therapy. The therapist listened, but also showed feelings of sorrow, and his expressing emotions helped give me self-confidence by conveying I was somebody worthwhile.

At the same time I became involved in a therapy group where we'd talk about things that were happening to us. I'd always been a good guy and never did anything wrong, but in some of these sessions I'd yell and scream and let out all this horrible unconscious stuff. I had to accept it, and realized I did have feelings. That was the beginning of my transformation. I started reading books on psychology, which was my first involvement in things deeper than the conscious.

I'd been a research scientist in my twenties and early thirties – a typical Five. It was through the struggle of my first marriage that I became more than just a normal Five, bringing emotional dimensions into my life. As painful as it was, my divorce was also liberating. I felt a certain amount of freedom because the relationship had been such a terrible block to my doing anything other than reacting to it.

The biggest lesson I learned from my divorce, besides realizing I have feelings, is that you need to share your strength as well as your compassion. You can't deal with some people kindly because they aren't going to be nice to you. I've been able to express myself more aggressively instead of withdrawing, although these experiences, especially explosive anger, have left me shaken.

I'm also aware of how my strength can be over-exercised. In my second marriage, I found myself living with an alcoholic, and became aware of my strength as a co-dependency issue. It wasn't one big insight, but it was definitely a shift over time to realize how I took care of things. I'm well aware of this issue in my life now and consciously try to deal with it, though it's kind of built into me. I think a lot about, *Shall I deliberately not try to fix this?* or, *I'll fix this, but it might be co-dependent.* I realize, for example, how I like to take care of my kids, and wonder, *Do I get involved too much? Do I not let them do enough, do I not make them live up to things?*

Hearing people in the Enneagram community talking about transformation has legitimized it for me, and given me a mental framework, the idea that the way to live is to somehow get away from personality. The Jungians say you need to have some contact with your unconscious to develop the Ego/Self axis – between your ego and your inner core. I like the whole intellectual idea you learn from the Enneagram, that we're living in some kind of – not really a dream – but some kind of unconscious activity, and to try to get away from that, to get out of being asleep.

In all cases, I've helped the process move by learning more about the subject relevant to my transformation. In most instances I joined groups to help me with new insights or ways of acting. In mid-life I went to T-groups, therapy groups, male-female workshops. More recently, I've attended Al-Anon, groups on Myers-Briggs and the Enneagram. I attend a weekly meditation group and have thought about doing Tai Chi – because the whole idea is getting out of my head, getting into other parts of my psyche, of who I am. I realized I was just thinking too much. My mind would race at night – I didn't have any trouble going to sleep, but I'd wake up in the middle of the night and I needed something to quiet my mind down.

I've also written down my dreams, trying active imagination. I use the Enneagram in a retrospective rather than a prospective way. For example, when I learned I was a Five, I looked back and realized I'd been able to engage with people and really enjoy it without revealing who I was myself, because I'd always been behind a screen of words. I assumed people didn't want to know about me. Now I reveal more, when I'm comfortable with someone. I can look for my generic Enneagram traits, noticing for example, *I'm probably too much in my head right now.*

I've boiled my resistances down to (1) skepticism, (2) not wanting to get involved in something new, and (3) having too many things on my plate to do so *I don't have time* for this activity.

I see the process of transformation as a Hero's Journey. You receive a call, you engage in the search, then there's a struggle, you have a breakthrough, and you return, somehow changed.

The call was particularly clear to me after retirement, when I'd been just living my life. A woman teaching a university course on personal development called and said she was leaving town and asked me to attend the following week to see if I'd be willing to take over for her. I took it as a call into the journey, because I thought *Why did I get a phone call out of the middle of nowhere, from someone I've never had contact with in my life, and who somehow knew there was a good chance I'd do it?* The request appealed to something inside of me. Something at an intuitive level, not verbal, said S*omething is going on here*, and I decided to try it out.

I could not believe the response of people taking that course – the warmth, and love. It's been great, wonderful! It's made these intellectual concepts more human. It's taken me outside my house and outside myself. And this is the way my life is going. The trick is to recognize it when it happens.

Commentary

The over-used gift of Style Five is to detach. It is their Ego's way of attracting attention. *Look at me, I'm above the fray, I don't get sucked in!* The two stories in this chapter illustrate when people rise above rising above and go beyond the stories their Egos are telling. Then the need to detach subtly transforms into something much, much more.

In these stories, transformation is "moving from one consistent and orderly psychic state to another more consistent and more integrated psychic state," as David notes. For Peter it is "similar to the notion of conversion – coming in possession of a quality that's a gift, that's beyond your own making." In these stories, their movements towards integration, moments of conversion lead to shifts of focus, so not only the cerebral transforms, but also integration of the rest of their person follows.

A common trait of people of Style Five is to live life in their heads and to compartmentalize experience. This can take the form of keeping different areas in life separate from each other, or it may involve keeping experience separate from the associated emotions. In the first story, Peter's sense of Ego relaxing was a series of experiences in which this compartmentalization between different areas in his life relaxed. He began by attending religious events just because his wife needed his presence so she could partake. Then, as Ego relaxed, he found benefit for himself. In a further step, he allowed this experience to flow into his job and inspire an unorthodox solution to an engineering problem that had addled the experts for weeks.

Ego relaxing that leads to an integration of emotional experience is a common theme in David's story. It took the ending of his first marriage to help him intellectually realize he didn't understand feelings. The next shift came in a therapy group where he began to accept his feelings, for him the start of his transforming.

People of Style Five are sometimes characterized as masters of minimalization. This is even reflected in what happens when Ego relaxes the strategy of striving to be detached. In these moments, a person of Style Five can experience the subtle shift from *Detachment* to the virtue of *Non-attachment*, which Jerry Wagner describes as "love expressed in an undulating ebb and flow. What comes in goes out; what has been freely received is freely given!"

This subtle shift is accompanied by a physical shift. As David puts it, "The whole idea is getting out of my head, getting into other parts of my psyche, of who I am." This shift allows him to share more of himself with others. In those moments he no longer needs to hide behind a screen of words.

Today Peter and David describe in similar terms how they move beyond the story Ego is telling. Transformation takes David outside his house and outside his self. "The trick is to recognize it when it happens." Peter notices when he's withdrawing into his little biosphere and, if he so chooses, leaves this container and become a contributor to and participant in life. Sometimes he puts himself in a place where grace can emerge – when it's the Inner Observer and not Ego operating. "I feel an at-easeness, a relaxation, where my body's not on edge. The best indicator for me is that I'm not attached to the outcome. Whatever happens is OK."

Three questions to ponder:

- How often do I take time to notice what's happening in my body?

- In what ways do my thoughts distract me from now?

- When do I confuse non-involvement with non-attachment?

Contents

1. Riding the Bull – Bill's story	85
2. Joy Moves It Along – Jim's Story	92
3. Commentary	97

Chapter Six – Style Six

Riding the Bull – Bill's story

To me the definition of *transformation* is in a quote from Suzanne Zuercher: "If our lives are to turn around, we need simply to acknowledge and admit our reality as it becomes known to us." I think that damn near says it all.

Most of the things I've learned have been from watching and listening to myself as my life unfolds. I look at what's provocative or what I don't have answers for, and as I continue to seek and to be open, the answers become apparent. I've concluded if you want to know, you keep that intention open over time, and clear away the space to listen, you're going to find out. It won't be overnight, and you may get layers and layers, and you may forget and come back. But I've not run into anything in my life where I've pushed for an answer that I haven't gotten it. I don't mean that makes me perfect, that I don't make mistakes. But answers come, and in strange places. It seems to be in fits and starts for me. I'm in a workshop and suddenly some stuff I've been working on pops up. Or I ask just the right question at just the right time and maybe a big scenario pops up.

I have to make space for that intention because I drift off. Unless I have something regular that brings me back I lose it, find myself down on the ground, out of my tree, into my defensive mode and my angry mode. It's almost like a compass. You pull the compass out and say, *Oh, my God, I'm off 30 degrees here. Where's North*? And then you find North and you swing back over and center yourself up again, you reconnect with whatever you've been working with. Mostly to me, when I think of tracking back on, it's simply getting in touch again with the truth about me that I know lies within. And it's being still enough and quiet enough long enough to allow that connection to be made.

However you've chosen to practice, it's that you practice. And I think we have to have some outside process on a regular basis. That could be an Enneagram workshop, it could be anything. But you need to go outside yourself to someone skilled in an area you're interested in, a like-minded group of people that extends over a period of time where you come in with the notion, *I am going to do some work*. You listen to other people doing some work, and there's interplay that tills the field, cross-fertilization that helps you get to a deeper place.

My once-a-week Al-Anon group works really well for me. I listen to these common, ordinary people who've got some things in their lives they're struggling with, coming out of a real place in real time, and it's helped me to find true North again.

I went to a workshop called *Riding the Bull Home*. That image is a good calibration for me. When I'm on the bull there's nothing to track. I'm moving down the path in a very carefree sort of way. *Carefree* is an important piece of that. Anything else is looking for the path. But I've spent very little time on the bull. Right now I see the path but I'm not on the bull. In some sense my whole life is a path, but there have been times when I was clearly looking to be on the path instead of being on it. I'm very comfortable with where I am right now and that comfort comes from being clear about what I'm trying to do, how I'm trying to live my life, and the progress I'm making. As I've worked with riding the bull I have found, to my surprise and my dismay and chagrin, it's enormously harder than I had any notion it would be.

An exercise during the workshop was to count your breaths for one hundred breaths, in breath and out breath, without an extraneous thought coming into your mind. Well, that seems so simple. It's impossible. But I've messed around with it long enough to get a glimmer it may well be true that if you control your mind, you control your life. And I guess I'd have to say, too, if you can't control your mind you're spitting into the wind if you say you're controlling your life, because it's simply not true.

Controlling your mind means having a task for it all the time. I learned from Robert Fritz's *The Path of Least Resistance* that we can choose to become the creative force in our lives. Its ultimate expression is that each moment, from moment to moment, I know what I'm about. I have a picture I want to create and I'm aware the action I'm taking is moving me in that direction. Now that's controlling your mind. While teaching yoga or meditation exercises in a no-smoking class, I have absolute, impeccable focus. So clearly my mind will do what I tell it to do, if I insist it stay with it. But given any sort of opportunity, my mind seems to take off. It occurred to me one day that I need an enormous amount of practice and I thought, *Well, let me look at some routine tasks I do in an ongoing, repetitive way. OK, a good one is brushing my teeth. It takes about three minutes max. I'll be really*

Chapter Six

aware of brushing my teeth for three minutes. Well I might get three seconds!

The enormous breakthrough in Enneagram terms was realizing I'm driven by fear. Before that, I was always aware that power was a big thing in my life, but I'd thought of it as *power*. I got in touch with the fact that yeah, it was a big thing in my life, but what made it a big thing was my being driven by *fear*. The difference is astronomical. You're not going to learn about fear by looking at power. You're going to learn about fear by looking at fear, by finding the fear within and welcoming and being open to the fear, accepting *Yeah, that's what it is, that's how it feels*. My life changed. No question. That was the transforming moment.

Knowing about *fear* opened some doors that had not been open before. It allowed me to understand what's going on with my current reality. It allowed me to understand a lot of things I could not understand before. The absolute bottom layer of fear in my life is the scenario that I'm a rabbit. Not a mouse. A rabbit. And rabbits have a lot of abilities, because they're food for many creatures and if they didn't have those abilities there wouldn't be any rabbits. The rabbit's fast, it has really good eyesight, good concealing ability, incredibly good hearing. It operates in a limited territory – about five acres – but the rabbit knows those five acres. So if danger is about, the rabbit is very likely to be aware there is danger. And it knows the actions it can take to avoid the dogs. The dogs are the environment out there. What I got in touch with is that when I'm in the clutches of fear, I believe everyone out there is faster than I am, smarter than I am, stronger than I am, and has more power than I have. On any kind of level ground, where there's one-on-one competition, I'm gone! So what I have to do is manage my five acres in such a way that one-on-one can never happen. And if you look at how that's set up, the better rabbit you are, the smarter you are, the more careful and alert you are, the longer you're going to last. But inevitably at some point you're going down! That's pretty heavy duty.

Oh, yeah. As I look back on my life to learn about this construct, I see that in all the modeling I got from my father, and we were on a farm so we did a lot of work together, he would always say, "OK, here's the way you do this." One time we'd borrowed a horse-drawn cultivator from one of the other farmers who could afford this kind of equipment, and I'd never seen one before. My father pulled it out to the edge of the front field, got on the thing, drove it fifty feet, showed me how to push the pedals, said, "That's the way you do that," handed me the reins, and left. And I got the hang of it and did the rest of the field. I could give you countless other examples but all of it was demonstration. There never was a time when he said, "There's a cultivator, go look at it and see if you can figure out how it works," or, "Let's sit down and talk about this and see what seems to make sense," never any notion of problem-solving, never "Hey, you're smart, and if you just think about it you'll come up with something that makes sense." My whole orientation was to find out what I was supposed to be doing.

Another example was when I was stationed in Korea, Officer of the Day, and was to close the Officer's Club and had to put the money away. I was 22 years old, a Second Lieutenant, never been over 20 miles from home. My orders and instructions were, "The Base Commander is the final authority on the base, and you're his representative. At 12 o'clock you close the Officer's Club and count the money." So I went in there at 12 o'clock, told the bartender to close the bar. And he said, "Well, the Deputy Commander wants to keep the bar open another 10 or 15 minutes." I pulled my pistol out, laid it on the bar, and said, "I want the bar closed. I'll be back in 10 minutes and when I get back I expect everybody to be gone, and we'll count the money." I came back in 10 minutes, everybody was gone. The next day the Base Commander called me over, kind of grinning, and said, "How'd things go?" I said, "They went fine." And he said, "I understand you closed the bar." I said, "Yeah, I did." He said, "Well, normally, if the Deputy wants to keep things open another 10 or 15 minutes that's probably OK." But it impressed the shit out of him that I closed the bar. A Second Lieutenant!

If there was a clear notion of what I was supposed to do then I always did incredibly well. If I didn't know what I was supposed to do, then I did not perceive if I simply thought about it I could figure out something that would make sense. Even now, the first thing that comes to mind is, *Oh, my God*! Sometimes it stays there, but normally I can say, *Oh, well, just calm down, be patient, see what this thing looks like*, and as I get more data coming in, things start looking fine. But still that fear is there, and I have a predisposition to do what people ask me to do. "Drop me off here?" "Yeah, I'll be glad to do that." I like to be helpful, but I'm concentrating right now on not saying, "Yes, I will do that," but to give information: "I'd really like to do that for you. Let me check and see what I have going on; and if it won't fit here, let's see if it will fit here." Saying yes automatically is fear I'll otherwise be thrown out of the group. It's also *These people are always stronger and smarter than I am, so it makes sense to stay on their good side.* But it's more of a group thing, really.

Anytime I feel a little fear I try to acknowledge it. Fear grabs a whole lot of my life. I've learned to appreciate the people who like to be out there, to break the trail, and can do that and do it well. In fact, an unexpected benefit to me of knowing the truth about what's going on with me is that life has become enormously more interesting. The quality of my existence has deepened and gotten much richer.

Before that awareness, my life was simpler and a lot more level. In my mid-twenties. I was an Adjutant Personnel Officer, and at the top of the heap, a First Lieutenant. I applied for a regular commission, went through ROTC, but didn't get approved for my regular commission. This surprised me because I'd decided to make the Air Force a career, so I thought *I've got to check this thing out.* I went to see the Lieutenant Colonel who was Director of Personnel and he said, "You're in a fairly soft career field. In a more critical field you wouldn't have any trouble. It looks like the two most critical fields available for you in the Air Force are electrical engineering and weather." Well, think about the disparity between electrical engineering and weather! I thought about it for about five seconds and said, "Let's go for electrical engineering."

That was exactly the way I chose the remaining 25 years of my Air Force life. What does that have to do with creating your own life? Not much! Once I'd gotten clear that I wanted to be a regular officer, I could sure as hell have given a little bit more thought to how I wanted to approach that. I had always liked people. As an Adjutant Personnel Officer my job was to take care of the people in the squadron, to make sure all the people business got handled. For all the administrative, payroll, supply, and barracks stuff, I was the final arbiter before we went to the Captain around discipline. And that was a perfect fit for me. I was really appreciated for it. When I left there to go to the school I'd applied for, this guy collected money as they did when an officer left, and he said, "The money just kept coming in!" It really broke me up.

The service was a good place for someone with my qualities at that time. They had regulations for everything. So there wasn't any question about how to do anything. I never really thought about myself until I got in the Creating course in my fifties. I knew I liked being around people, working with people but most of my focus was on getting the job done.

My experience says if you want to know, without reservation, the truth cannot be kept from you. You will find it. But I wonder what percentage of people really do want to know, with that intensity, over that period of time, and keep on wanting to know when they see some pretty heavy stuff! That's why I said to put yourself in group situations on a regular basis, even if you don't perceive, *Oh, I need to work on this*. You need to throw yourself into the water and have a few layers unravel. And the sooner you can see, the better off you are. It's amazing to me how I was able to keep some of these things from myself. Sometimes I'm elated, and sometimes it just feels like, *Oh shit, another deep, heavy piece of work I've got to do*. I get depressed about *It's still there and it's still holding me back*. The thing I'm feeling good about is that I'm being pretty good to myself. I don't mean I don't track off, or get depressed. It's hard for me to keep the stress down sometimes. I still get caught up in worrying about my daughter, worrying about my wife, worrying about my mechanic!

A concluding thought here is that the Twelve Step program helped me codify the notion of a Higher Power. It brought me to an enormously helpful realization I'd not had before, that as I look at my life as a whole, I'm clear I've mismanaged a lot of it. And I don't mean I've screwed up. I'm just saying if I had been in touch with this information stream from my Higher Power, things would have gone better, and easier, and the quality of my life would have been greatly enhanced if I'd sooner thought not just *I need help with this*, but *I need help!* I had never really thought about my life like that. It allowed me to get to a different place around the management of my life and at the same time reinforced the notion that everyone else has their Higher Power, too, and they sure as hell don't need me to run their life! It got me down another level where I know absolutely, irrevocably, I can't be responsible for someone else's life because I don't know what's good for them.

The tools I've found incredibly helpful are first, the notion of Creating in its purest form, second the Enneagram, third the DISC, and fourth the Twelve Step program. Each one of those tools allows me to get a grip on some things in my life I don't think I could have gotten without it. Each shows you some things the others have not shown. And there are tools and tools and tools. So keep exploring, keep looking for them, keep listening to other people, find the right ones for you and use them.

    The quote I started with is the key. I honestly believe if anyone wants to see the truth about what's going on in their life – totally, objectively, non-judgmentally – and stay with it, their life is going to change. If I'm there waiting to see, eventually I am going to see it.

Joy Moves It Along – Jim's Story

One of my friends told me several times you can't fundamentally change – all you can do is change your behavior. I argued that point with him, but I don't have to argue it anymore. I think transformation is profound change, to the point where you never want to go back.

I recognized I had to change a long time ago, for my own well-being as well as for those around me. I've been yearning for this for a long time. I just never found a way to do it. Frankly, when I first looked at Mary [Bast]'s web site I thought, *My God, this is some sort of cult!* It's that funny diagram – *What the heck is that?* Then I read what she wrote about a counterphobic Six, and I began to recognize that part of the reason my company hadn't been successful in our new venture was because I put my partners on the defensive with my tendency to state my objections in such a blunt and often challenging way. I was so furious once about someone we'd hired, the President looked at me and said, "You know, I'm worried about you; you're angry and accusing beyond anything that's called for." He was brave to say that because usually I'd defend my position, fight to the death. That bothered me and I began to examine my own contribution to our lack of progress toward our strategic objectives, our ineffectiveness as a leadership group. I said, *This has got to change, for two reasons: I can't keep acting like this, and we're not effective.*

I'd made substantial changes earlier in my marriage, but these changes weren't so far-reaching. I'd complained a lot, and could be sarcastic. It was just the way I expressed myself. But I realized if I didn't make any changes at home I was going to lose my marriage, and I began a real campaign to do something about it. I think that was fairly profound, but I never carried it outside my marriage. I didn't care what other people thought about me. I was going to go get the job done, and fuck 'em if they didn't like the way I did it!

At first I thought I was an Eight. I read in Goldberg's *The Nine Ways of Working* that "Eights see black or white, friend or foe, strong or weak, likeable or not," and I saw those extremes in me. I was bothered by my anger, and by what my anger did to people, including me. I probably took minutes or hours off my life every time I lost it. However, Goldberg's statement that "Eights are apparently guilt-free," didn't resonate at all. Along with the desire to change, I've carried tremendous guilt that I wasn't able to change effectively, or wasn't making any progress, or would revert. But I didn't have any real clue as to how to keep it going.

I used to dominate a conversation with nervous talk, but coaching sessions have taught me to look at somebody and listen to them and not to be in a hurry to overwhelm them with my answer. What happened to me this weekend was unbelievable. We had two huge training sessions, and from the minute I stood up in front of that 90-person group I felt different about them, what I was going to say, and how I was going to say it. I never paid any attention before to how people responded to me. But I watched their response and I found myself letting people answer their own questions.

Afterwards, one guy stuck out his hand, and said, "Wasn't this a really great weekend?" I had to get in the car and put my dark glasses on. There were a lot of people standing around and I wasn't going to let them see the tears.

This is so overwhelming, I don't even know how to think about it. I keep getting different responses in people. And I walk away from conversations with a different view of what happened because I've paid attention to how the person is responding to me. I'm far more relaxed. I used to get so upset over little things. Just this morning I went in the garage to put some stuff into the trunk of my car and the trunk was locked. My reaction earlier would have been, *Goddamn it! Why is the trunk locked*? But this morning I just thought, *Oh, the trunk is locked*, and I walked around to the door and unlocked the trunk. This is the sort of thing that happens to me all the time now. I don't know where my irritability went, all that pointing of fingers at other people.

One result is that I'm having so much more fun. A year ago someone told me, "You never smile," and I've thought about that a lot recently. I was anxious, uptight because I didn't want to show it. Now I find myself smiling all the time. *Pleasant* doesn't even begin to describe how that feels.

When I first talked to a therapist about my anger he said, "Ah, that's OK. You're doing fine." Here he was sitting across from me and I'm saying, "I really get angry, SO WHAT!!!!" What the hell was he going to say? The next counselor I saw was not by choice either. The President of that company said, "You go get some help or you're out of here." But also, I was very dissatisfied where I was. I could do superb work but that was offset by my relationships with other people, my tendency to light into people who didn't follow the ground rules. So this time the work with the counselor was good, but we just scratched the surface. We never got into the soul of what was going on. It was more techniques. For example, I'd put Post-It stickers on my dashboard to remind myself if something occurred I ought not to lose my temper. And it worked until the Post-it fell off, as they always do – you know, things aren't permanent. And the next thing you knew, I was pissed off at some old lady who was in my way. It was a series of Band-Aids and I don't say that was bad, but it wasn't very satisfying, it wasn't getting me where I wanted to go.

Yet I knew I needed to make the profound change. I had no knowledge of the Enneagram, no idea I'm a Six, no idea where the journey would go or how to even start. I knew I had to change for my own good, for my marriage, for my job, whatever – probably mostly for my own good – but I didn't know how to do it.

What's so awesome about this to me is that for some reason I had absolute, almost child-like, unqualified trust in Mary, so I took what she said and I went in that direction, and I don't know why. Maybe it's because I had so many years of being ready to do this without having the roadmap to do it, but I also think you can't be questioning or fighting with the person who's helping you. I marvel at two things: First, that I've been able to continue the process as profoundly as I have, and secondly, I don't care where it ends. It's a kind of surrender, which is very interesting, because growing up a Christian Scientist, one of the fundamental notions was, *yield to God's will* and I always resisted that. I mean, "Nobody's going to tell me what to do!" The notion of spirituality has gained a significance for me I don't think it's ever had. What I've done here is yield to something that has let me change. There's this incredible sense of peace, and I've started praying. A lot of my prayer is just thanks, but part of it is recognition that there is some sort of spiritual force – relinquishing the notion that there's nothing out there or that it won't help us.

Among the techniques I learned to help stay conscious, I like Gendlin's Focusing. The interesting part about Focusing is that you're not self-condemning, you're simply noting. When I understood that, it was easy. It's tied to what I was saying before about yielding. You've got to accept it's the right thing and go with it. And I don't have to sit there and think about what I'm doing. Focusing taught me how to be

Chapter Six

where I wanted to be anyway. I also read more about my Enneagram style. I can go back, look at the behaviors of a Six, recognize how that relates to me and what I can do about it. The oddest part is that I haven't had to sit here and plot some kind of change. It has just sort of unfolded in front of me, and that has continued to awe me, the notion of yielding and letting it happen.

Self-disclosure is something I haven't been reluctant about, once I figured out I needed to change. I had looked at myself for a long time. On one hand I was pretty objective, and on the other hand I was self-condemning. The objectivity is fine, but I've learned that self-condemning is a major impediment to change. That's the gorilla I've been wrestling with, and you don't easily get that off of your shoulders. But when I look at positive responses to the changes in me from people I'd treated pretty badly, it's so rewarding that I've begun to say to myself, *Get off the guilt trip. There's nothing you can do about it now, other than changing your current behavior.* And I think I've made progress. I used to beat myself up pretty badly. I beat myself up about things I did to my wife. And I don't know that the pain of recollecting that is ever going to go away. I don't know if I'm ever going to be able to say, *It was all right.* I think I have more work to do there. If you want the ultimate transformation, it would probably be to let go of that.

If I sat here and tried to model this, I probably could, but that would seem artificial to me. My experience of the process is more intuitive, diffuse, emotion-laden. It's joy that moves it along. I don't know if it has stages. I didn't spiral into this, I didn't go up steps, I didn't go down steps, there's been no fight here. It's a process that goes on without conscious thought in my case. I'm not struggling or trying. I still find it amazing that I don't have to go through the great labor I'd been enduring for years. Whatever it was that was blocking this change hasn't fought back very effectively recently. Maybe it was tired. Maybe I'd beat that little mother to death!

One of the things I've asked is, "Where am I going with all of this?" I've gone through life always having to know where I was going; otherwise I wasn't going to do it. I mean, why would we start if we aren't going someplace we'd defined and we knew? But I got to thinking that asking where I'm going supposes there is an end point, and I'm not sure I want to define an end point. Probably the most important part of all this is the continuing recognition that transforming makes sense, that it's *right*, and just to continue the process.

Commentary

The overused gift of Style Six is to be secure. It is their Ego's way of attracting attention – look at me (but not too much), I'm secure. Nothing can go wrong, if Ego remains vigilant, dutiful, and loyal. The two stories in this chapter illustrate what can happen when people move beyond the stories their Egos are telling. Then they transform the need to be secure into something much richer.

In the first story, transformation is best described for Bill by a Suzanne Zuercher quote: "If our lives are to turn around, we need simply to acknowledge and admit our reality as it becomes known to us."

For Jim, in the second story, it is "profound change, to the point where you never want to go back."

A common trait of people of Style Six is to exhibit counterphobic behavior, when striving to be secure. Jim's story contains many examples where this took the form of being aggressive towards others. This behavior led to him jeopardizing that which provided him with the security in his life: marriage, job and friendships. As his boss said, "You know, I'm worried about you; you're angry and accusing beyond anything that's called for."

Bill's behavior, like many of Style Six, was driven by Fear. Simply realizing this was an enormous breakthrough for him. Previously he had been aware that power was a big topic in his life. The shift came when he realized its size was being driven by fear. Then he switched focus to learning about, welcoming and accepting fear.

In moments when Ego relaxes, a person of Style Six can experience *Courage*, which Jerry Wagner describes as "the virtue that follows naturally from the disposition of faith. Courage is not a freedom from fear but entails the freedom to act in the face of fear. Derived from the Latin and later the French word for heart, *cor* or *couer*, courage is the attitude of facing and dealing with anything recognized as dangerous, difficult, or painful instead of withdrawing from it." In the first story, Bill describes this as *riding the bull home*, the name of a workshop he attended. When his Ego relaxes, he moves along life's path in a carefree manner. With this comes clarity and comfort.

For Jim courage takes the form of being more relaxed. His story is a chain of events that illustrate how the Serenity Prayer can unfold in someone's life. Everyday upsets no longer phase him; when he meets a locked trunk, he just notes it's locked and opens it, rather than reacting with *Goddamn it! Why is the trunk locked!*

This unfolding path is leading to a deeper and richer life in which he experiences the higher quality of *Faith*. When he reached his rock bottom, when he realized he had to change for his own good and that of his marriage and job, he didn't know how to do it. Then the act of faith came when he surrendered and placed a childlike, unqualified trust in working with Mary. He began to yield to something and this let him change. Today he recognizes that ongoing transformation makes sense.

Bill uses different tools to help him ride his bull home. The Enneagram helped him recognize the central role fear plays in his life, to realize when he's *off 30 degrees here*, to equip him to reconnect with what he knows to be the truth about himself and come back on track. It's an unexpected benefit that life has become enormously more interesting, deeper and richer. As he says, "I honestly believe that if anyone wants to see the truth about what's going on in their life – totally, objectively, non-judgmentally – and stay with it, their life is going to change. If I'm there waiting to see, eventually I am going to see it."

Three questions to ponder:

- To what or where do my thoughts tend to race?

- To which practice(s) have I committed and how do I notice their impact?

- How do I notice ways my innate faith plays out in my life?

Contents

1. Mosaic – Jessica's story   101

2. Altered States – Alan's Story   112

3. Commentary   120

Chapter Seven – Style Seven

Mosaic – Jessica's story

For me, transformation is about things becoming different, and a mosaic is one of the metaphors I've used, especially since my husband's death – the cause of my greatest transformation so far. My life as I knew it was shattered, and in this healing process it's being put back as something completely different. In life's mosaic you might not recognize some pieces, but they can be put together in infinite combinations.

For me there is work in transformation. So the mosaic is both what I'm creating and what's coming into creation, in that I don't think I created some of those experiences in my life – I certainly didn't create my husband's dying – but it is what I have to work with: *So what am I going to do with those pieces? What are they going to look like*? And especially since that experience, I'm much more open to going *Hmmm... more exciting if I have no idea. We'll see.*

As I approached the third anniversary of his death, someone asked, "Does it seem like it was just yesterday?" And I said, "No, it seems, actually, like it was about six lifetimes ago, because so many different things have happened in that time. So it's that kind of a mosaic. When you look at one section it looks like something, but when you pull further back or you move further down, you see that was actually part of something bigger.

The first major shift in my life happened when I went from southern California to Minnesota to college, having never visited the town. I just wanted to get the hell out of my parents' house. I read some literature but had no clue what I was getting into. The college town was a good-sized community of 10,000 people. I'd come from the L.A. metro area and thought I knew everything about the world, but I met all sorts of people I knew almost nothing about.

One of the first days of school someone said they were from Cambridge and I said, "Oh really? Massachusetts?" and they said, "No, Cambridge, Minnesota," really taking offense, like how could I not know? I felt so self-conscious, like I didn't get the script. I hadn't really studied in high school though I was able to get OK grades. But some of the other students were merit scholars and valedictorian of their class.

I was so used to being with people who'd had similar experiences. So to go to school there was the first real recognition of differences, and it was also the beginning of being out of my parents' home and trying to figure out who I was.

I used to say I grew up in the family of Ordinary People, where everything looked good on the outside. My parents were upper-middle-class, church-going people who provided for all our needs, but emotionally there was chaos and conflict. My mother was an active alcoholic and my dad worked all the time. I often felt I couldn't understand what was going on. I didn't know then about alcoholism, I just thought that's how life was. But I did know I was incredibly lonely in my family. And I created family outside my family, friends from church and high school. When the same friends would say, "I wish I had your parents." I asked myself *How could that be*? but I never said anything because I thought it was about me, that I didn't appreciate my parents. My sister had an eating disorder, and my brother had a lot of anger issues. So I was that middle kid who tried to get along.

There were definitely similarities in my college experience: *Gosh, how is it that everyone else seems to know what's going on and says it's OK, but it doesn't feel OK to me*? So that was one of those times when I saw how I used my outgoing, friendly, humorous piece – to try to make up for all the discord that was inside. I only lasted there a year. By January I wanted to leave school because it was 40 degrees below zero, and I hadn't gotten good grades because I didn't know how.

I stayed until May. That was it. Then I said I'd take some time off and figure out what I wanted to do with my life. Both of my parents had gone to college and there was no question about going to college; it was just a matter of where you went. So I said, "I'll find someplace to go, starting in September." And I did. That's how I ended up going to a small Lutheran school. I spent my last semester of college in Mexico, just outside of Mexico City and Cuernavaca, as part of a Global Juice and Peace program through another university. There were 14 students living in community in this house where we did some Spanish immersion. Then I spent two weeks in Nicaragua and studied Latin American history and politics.

I'd been very influenced by a pastor who came to the church I'd grown up in who'd been a missionary in Bogota, Columbia and was involved in liberation theology and peace and justice issues. Working with him and then going on this trip really changed my world view. I became aware not only of how my family pretended everything was OK, but that I lived in a country where everyone else looked that way, too. I could see there were people who didn't live like this at all. I stayed with a family for about two weeks where there were only two beds in the house. One was for the parents, and I was never really clear who else lived in the house, but they let me have one of the two beds. Only two of the rooms actually had paved floors. I hadn't known people lived like this day after day, and also – in the midst of that – they had lives. That was very transforming.

When I then went to seminary in Minnesota, 50 miles from where I'd gone to college, I had changed. While I'd lived in Mexico I was determined to have the fullest experience possible, and I decided I wanted to do that when I went back to Minnesota. So not only had the experience heightened my sense of my place in a greater global community, but also it gave me different eyes to see more of the things we have in common, being open to new experiences.

I spent four years in Minnesota and one year in Wisconsin, and during that whole time in the mid-west my experience was very different from that first year. I made good friends, I figured out how to navigate the cold weather. That's continued to be a reminder for me: when I feel I'm out of my element, instead of running away from it or becoming defensive, to embrace it and say, "Well, if I were in Mexico, what would I be doing?" That served me very well when I had my first congregation in rural Montana.

But in between, I spent four years in the seminary, immersed in theological education, and had an experience that was enlightening and powerful. I got into therapy and into recovery – because I saw a therapist who recognized me as the child of an alcoholic and would not see me if I didn't go to a Twelve Step meeting every week. In the second year in the seminary, to continue you have to be matriculated – it's how they weed people out of the program – and my professor had said "I'll stop your matriculation if you don't go see a therapist." My back was against the wall.

Once when a small group of us were processing our visits to a hospital for a nursing home, one of my professors had said, "I wonder if you think in black and white terms, if you ever experience seeing things differently from how other people see them? I think you've grown up in an alcoholic family and I think you need some help. You're making up stories about things." I didn't know the difference between

103

what was true and what I imagined. And in this class we were doing pastoral visits to people in hospitals and nursing homes. It was about being fully present; and I was incapable of that.

I was devastated, felt kind of found out, and also afraid if my defense mechanisms fell apart – all my pretending everything was OK – what would I do? Yet what he said was significant, because it got me into therapy and into Al-Anon. My final year at school I became his teaching assistant and I was so grateful for everything he'd done for me, for speaking the truth about what was broken in my life.

The first assignment the therapist gave me was to spend half an hour by myself every day – not watching TV, not talking to people, not exercising – just being there. I went back the next week and said, "I couldn't do it." So she suggested spending 15 minutes by myself, and I was able, over time, to be with me. If I couldn't be with myself, how could I be with other people? I think that's what my professor saw.

During my senior year in the seminary I was involved with a man who was older, who'd come to the seminary as a second-career student after being in the advertising industry. I thought I was in love with him and didn't want to move out of the Queen City area because he'd still be in school, so thought I'd go to one of the areas within reasonable distance from the seminary. The Bishops all got together to assign maybe 350 graduates across the country, and it was kind of an NFL draft thing where they bargained for different people. I found out I was being sent to southern California where I grew up, not in Wisconsin where I'd requested.

One of my professors said "Aren't you excited?" And I said "No." And he said, "A lot of people wanted you. This is one of the best places to be. You were one of the first people picked." And that was so like the family I grew up in. I felt I couldn't say it wasn't what I wanted. I just couldn't figure out what to do, so took a year off. The same professor who'd gotten me into therapy had an experimental program exploring what it would look like to have people from different backgrounds – medicine, religion, social work, education – do a part-time therapy immersion experience. We all had Master's degrees. We'd read books on family therapy and actually conduct therapy. But it was an expensive program, and I was working at 3M as a temporary office person in their legal department, and couldn't afford to do both.

My relationship had ended, and in one of those spur-of-the-moment things I thought, "Fine, I'm just going to get a congregation and I don't care where I go." But I didn't want to go back to southern California because it would be too close to my parents. One of my professors said "I can't believe you're not in a parish, you're so wonderful, blah blah blah," and when I told him I was thinking of looking for a parish, he asked if I'd be interested in going to Montana. I said, "OK" and within two months I was interviewing in Montana. That's where I drew on my experience in Mexico, wanting to get the most out of it, and it was a big ego experience as well. In the seminary, if you were one of the top candidates you'd be seen as going to one of the more desirable parishes, and if you were someone they thought couldn't do much damage, they'd send you to North Dakota. So I thought *Isn't this great of me? I'm one of the top people, and I'm going to one of the worst places.* It was one of those icky fake humility things.

That was a big growing experience as well. I was associate pastor to someone who couldn't find another job and the relationship was tumultuous. It got me doing the Twelve Step program, working harder in therapy exploring myself, and that's when I met my husband. I was called to a multi-point parish where my husband had served an internship six years earlier. Part of my initial job description was getting a youth program up and running, so he and I began talking on the phone about it. I was very quickly in over my head, difficulties with a colleague and people needing a lot of help. I wasn't always capable of saying no to them or figuring out whether to do the best I could or provide nothing. There were no social services in that small, unhealthy town. I was 26 years old and pastor to a young man who'd been hired at a youth ranch and then discovered to be a pedophile, and pastor also to members of my congregation who were threatening to kill him!

I found refuge in talking to this man who became my husband. When I met him it was as if I'd known him for a long time, and he was different from anyone I'd ever dated. He asked me to be part of a meeting and go out to dinner afterwards. Six weeks after that dinner we were engaged. If we'd been counseling another couple we'd have said "Date for six months, and then we'll get back to you." So we decided to seek a pastor colleague to do pre-marital counseling with us. I was still seeing a therapist who, after my leaving the bad relationship, had asked me to agree to spend a year without dating anyone. That got me out of the pattern of choosing people like my mom. If they weren't actually alcoholics, which some of them were, they were subject to rages. So my husband was someone who, years before, I wouldn't have noticed because he was so calm.

After I learned the Enneagram we used to joke that "Nines start off slow and taper from there." It was true of him. So he was a great complement to my personality. There were times when he would have said he was more invested in our marriage than I was. That was probably true. He did more things to be connected. I'm not a memento person, but I pulled out something recently that made me smile. For our first Christmas after we were married he'd bought a Hallmark ornament with two raccoons on it, inscribed "It's our first Christmas together!" That kind of thing is so not my style. But I loved that it was his style. He was the one who liked movies like "You've Got Mail!" Especially early on, that kind of direct expression of emotion was still very uncomfortable for me.

He'd been diagnosed with Hodgkin's Lymphoma when he was 26 years old and told he had less than six months to live. I met him when he was 31. The connection he had with his congregation was very intense because he'd only been there a year-and-a-half when he had to say, "I can't get the kind of treatment I need for the cancer here and I don't know if I'll be back." His parents had taken him on his "last" trip, he came back and had radiation; then his prognosis looked pretty good. Two friends who'd gone through seminary with him both had died of Hodgkin's, which confirmed for him he'd been given a second chance. So he'd returned to his congregation in Montana with enthusiasm and renewed love of life. Yet he agreed to leave this congregation he'd served for seven years because we lived 300 miles apart. The wedding shower they gave us was the most depressing one I'd ever been to, because they were so disappointed to lose him.

He told me before we married that Hodgkin's has a very high recurrence rate and I really had to think *Do I want to do this*? But I loved him and was so grateful to have met him. When I decided I couldn't take Montana anymore and was called to a big church with a very large congregation, we had a trip to England planned. I said, "Oh, we can't go because there'll be moving expenses," and he said, "You only live once." He was always open to trying out new things.

I think this was the beginning of what would become a couple of pretty quick changes in my perception of the world, from *I see the world not as it is but as I am*. I was 30 years old and everyone was saying, "Oh, I can't believe you're at this big church!" It was televised every week. I had all this external stuff, and internally I absolutely hated it and felt trapped. I told a friend, "I can't figure this out. It seems whatever job I've had, in so many different areas – I've been a camp counselor, I've worked at a card store, I've been a temporary in a legal department, I've been a pastor – the same irritating people keep showing up wherever I work!" Well, they were always so demanding! So picky about stuff. So serious about things! Fortunately, this friend had the audacity and the courage to ask, "Have you ever thought the common factor might be you?" I heard it, and thought, "It is. And I'm not going to wait for this situation to change. It's going to have to be me who changes."

That same year I read Bernie Siegel's *Love, Medicine, and Miracles*, and I came home from working at a fundamentalist Christian camp for kids and told my husband, "I'm quitting my job so I don't get cancer!" We were leaving the next day to go to Florida on vacation and he said, "Why don't we talk about it while we're on vacation?" I said "I don't want to do it one more day." I agreed I'd stay through the end of December, but at this point my husband was only partly employed because there'd been a church in crisis and the bishop asked him to fill in, but his job was going to end and we'd bought a house nine months before, so I was pretty much the income earner, the one who had the insurance, the one with the more stable job. And I wanted to quit it. Once again my husband said "Absolutely. We'll figure it out." I wanted to do something more like the family therapy I'd done, so I told the bishop "I don't think this is the right career for me, I'm at a crisis point, and I need a break." He said they'd find something for my husband at a place that would work. So I went to get a Master's in Counseling at the University of South Dakota and my husband took a church nearby.

My son was born in October of 1993 and I was scheduled to start my counseling program in January. I completed that degree in two-and-a-half years while my son was an infant and then a little kid. We didn't have much money because I was a student and my husband was in a rural congregation. We lived in a house owned by the church. I would take classes when my husband could watch our son or he'd drive 30 miles to the university so I could nurse the baby, so we co-parented a lot.

We'd been married fifteen years when he died of a stroke, not from lymphoma after all. We now understand he had the stroke because of a blood clotting disorder that's been diagnosed in our daughter. We didn't know it at the time, and I wouldn't have known it if I hadn't taken my daughter to the doctor for all her bloody noses.

Prior to my husband's death I'd say the biggest transformation for me was my son's birth, because so many of my family issues were right there for me. I had an emergency C-section, the baby came out crying and didn't stop for months and months. He was a very colicky, challenging baby and I was in a remote part of South Dakota with no one I could relate to. People would say things like "You're a nervous mother. If you weren't so nervous he'd be a better baby." Fifteen years later what I couldn't let in then makes sense to me now: that my son has sensory integration issues. Some people think it's part of being bipolar, and he wasn't diagnosed as bipolar until he was eight years old. So from his birth to age eight, I was pretty clear that I was an incompetent parent and that was why he was how he was.

My daughter was born when he was four, and I took her to the pediatrician when she was two years old because she only had about a hundred words and I thought she was delayed. My son was speaking in full sentences by the time he was two. But he was also emotionally volatile and became violent. He hit his teacher when he was in kindergarten because she'd tapped him unexpectedly on the back. He turned around and punched her, then came home and said "The teacher was trying to hurt me." Also my husband had decided to take a suburban church outside Denver and we'd moved to Colorado. He'd been there two-and-a-half-years when they decided they'd open up a congregation to work with the women's prison in Denver. So at the time when my son's behavior was getting tougher, my husband was in the middle of being trained to be a pastor inside prison walls. My husband and I had done most of the parenting together and he'd always been the go-to person if something was too much for me. But he was gone. That was one of the toughest times of my life.

My husband loved sports, loved TV, following his teams, watching the NCAA. Once, when it was a really hard time with his congregation, he came home from work looking really down and I said, "Gosh, isn't all this getting to you?" and he said, "Yeah, the Broncos didn't make the play-off and it doesn't look like the Rockies are going to have a good season!" Our son could name every single team of the NHL and their logos when he was two years old. This was his "twice-exceptional" piece they talk about now – very, very gifted and mentally ill. He read before he went to kindergarten and no one had taught him. So it was a wake-up call when he was diagnosed as bipolar and the doctor said, "You're delusional. What haven't you noticed about this child?"

When he was seven years old, he'd get mad and push at the teacher. I'd go in by myself to the school office, to see the principal, to have conferences with the school social worker, because my husband was gone a lot, and they'd say, "How do you discipline him at home? How much other violence is there in your home?" I realized, *Gosh, they think I abuse this kid.* So at this point – and this is now the key for me that my compulsion is going to kick in – I felt I was in over my head. I told my husband, "You've got to take over from here; I can't do this anymore." So he stepped in, arranged his calendar so he could go to the parent-teacher conferences, to the principal's office, and they'd say, "You are the best dad!" He was a pastor in the community and had that quiet presence and confidence.

Part of me wanted to walk out. I imagined telling my husband I was going for a long drive and changing my identity. Fortunately, a woman at the Al-Anon meetings I'd been going to regularly talked about her 19-year-old son who was an addict, how she'd walked out when he was four years old, now she was back and it was so much work! My son was four at the time, and I thought *If I walk out, she is my future.* I was very, very grateful to her. One of the ways I think of my life and experiences, and also a spiritual perspective for myself, is being "God's great recycling plan." It's the trash, the stuff we want to throw away, that is so useable. Because it always, always seems that someone later would be going through what I'd already been through.

Growing up in a family where my mother was an alcoholic Three and my father a Seven, among my ways of resisting things is the external make-over. *Let's just put on a new coat of paint and it will all be OK* instead of taking the time to dig deeper. I have 20 years of written journals in my closet, which has really helped with my questioning, *Is that real?* When I'd tell a story and then wonder *Did I just make that up?* I could go back and find it historically. Journaling has also helped because sometimes I'd read back about something that had upset me and I wouldn't even know who the people were who'd upset me so much! I had a poster with a quote from Simon Wiesenthal, who founded the Museum of Tolerance: "Hope lives when people remember." That's been my motivation for both the practice of journaling and my practice of sitting quietly at the beginning of the day.

When I remove myself from being in the present moment, my life is absolutely unmanageable. But in Twelve Step recovery we say "we practice spiritual progress, not spiritual perfection." And the progress for me has been that I'm more often in the moment. I'm much more likely to pause when something is difficult, as a way of staying with it; whereas before I used to fight with things. If it was hard, I'd work harder. *I'll make a list. I'll fix it.* So another form of resistance is busyness. I own a part-time organizing business and see how people struggle with rearranging things on the outside trying to solve core problems. It doesn't work. You have to solve the core problem; you can't just rearrange the furniture.

If I were to distill my life's transformational points, they were always in heart-to-heart connections, whether it was about the healing piece with the family I grew up in, or finding my own identity and working on healing my own heart, or marriage, or parenting, or death. Seeing the Enneagram through the centers, it's been work around healing the heart center and using it for its correct purpose. I'm being intentional about using my feeling center, expanding it on things that can reciprocate, whereas before I'd use my thinking center – I'd have intellectual relationships with people, not intimate relationships.

When my husband died, he'd had the flu and was throwing up. We now know with his blood-clotting disorder you can throw blood clots when you get highly dehydrated. He had a stroke at our house in the morning before I went to work. He was unconscious but regained consciousness. We were an eighth of a mile from the hospital, so the ambulance took him to the hospital and the doctors said "He's within the three-hour window so let's give him this blood-thinner and we can hope for a full recovery." With his disorder, which we didn't know about, that was the very thing they shouldn't have done. As the day progressed he didn't get better, I stopped in the chapel and said, *You know what, God, if he's going to die, take him now. I cannot take months of rehabilitation, only to have him die.* There were phone calls in the night that he was unconscious and they'd put in a breathing tube. Because of my work in long-term care I knew I was not going to leave in a breathing tube, but his family is fundamentalist Christian and believed pulling the plug like that was evil, so I was so glad he and I had had many conversations about this and I knew it was what he'd want. He died within 10 minutes after it was removed.

People started coming in for his funeral and reaching out to us, saying "Oh my God, what's going to happen, he was the primary income earner and didn't have much insurance," and I said "You know what? I'm not worried about the money. I'm grateful because we have spiritual resources to draw on." In this encapsulated moment I thought, *All this work I've done on my life; here it is*! I had kind of a surreal feeling; I knew God didn't do this to me. That was my most transformational moment.

And I have incredible gratitude for the Enneagram, which had been introduced to me four years before my husband's death. I thought *This is a matter of the heart. The heart hasn't been the strongest place for me as a Seven, so I'm going to get it on my radar that I'd better keep working with my heart*. His death would have been the perfect reason for *Let's just pretend it's all OK*. In the years since, the Enneagram for me has been like the CliffsNotes, because it highlights what's most important. I don't want to shut down my heart. I also think, in conjunction with the mosaic metaphor, when my heart keeps breaking it gets to have more room. It's when hearts break that they start to expand.

Altered States – Alan's Story

My transformation has been in ideas about what is, learning something that all of a sudden convinced me, *I thought I knew and I really didn't and there's a way to learn it.* I'm an intellectual in both the good and bad senses of that term. I haven't studied physics or chemistry or biology. I've studied ideas. My father was a Five and I have a strong connection to Five. I *really* live in my head. The pattern has been that I've changed before I let myself see I needed to change. Then after I changed I knew I needed to have changed that.

I'll give you some examples. When I was 19 I went to dinner with the local priest and his friend who was an artist. At one point his friend looked at the door and said, "God that's an ugly door." I looked at the door and thought to myself, *I didn't know doors could be ugly or beautiful*! The whole meal they talked about things I didn't know existed. The next week I entered college because I wanted to know what they knew.

When I'd taken my exam to enter the railroad a couple of years before that, the word got through that I had the highest IQ of anybody who'd ever applied for a job with the railroad. So I assumed I was really on top of the world. Then I went to college and got my first D. I didn't know what the hell to do. I went to the teacher and he said, "Here's what you do; you actually read the book!" The book was Huckleberry Finn, which I'd read as a kid ten years before and figured *I don't have to read that because I've already read it.* He asked for "spot" passages – I had no idea such a thing existed.

It was brand new that I had to work to get through school because I hadn't taken a book home during high school. I was really a rube. There were only four kids in my high school graduating class, only 19 in the whole school, and most of them were farm boys who had to work as soon as they got home. They never read anything, even their assignments. I didn't know you had to study to get A's.

And then one morning, at 11:30 on a Tuesday in front of the post office – this is kind of spooky – I entered an altered state. I'd been struggling, and all of a sudden I *knew*, with an unshakable confidence that stays with me today, I was going to be a good philosopher and theologian. Whatever that took, I was going to do it. And after that experience I was on the honor roll and graduated in the top four percent of my class.

I've had a number of those altered states. I was 16 the first time it happened, the day school was to start for my senior year in high school. It was early September and already getting chilly. We were so poor I had only one new piece of clothing for school and I was wearing my new red sweatshirt, which felt really good on me. I was on the east side of the house, out of the cool wind and in the warm sun, and all of a sudden went into an altered state, an experience of being absolutely confident and calm and integrated. I knew everything was going to be all right.

Then a year or two later I started working on the railroad. I had never eaten at a restaurant or been away from home overnight; that's how small and totally integrated my world was. I'd been away from home only a few weeks, and I was dreadfully homesick. Just sick! So I thought *I'm going to make myself happy. I'm only going to eat what I like.* I hadn't had my first ice cream until I won a spelling contest in the sixth grade. The teacher gave me 15 cents to buy an ice cream sundae, and I thought this was the most wonderful thing in the world. Then in high school, after basketball games, I would have a chocolate malted milk. This was a really, really big deal. So when I was lonesome in this town I thought, *I'm just going to have chocolate malted milk.* I had malteds for breakfast, lunch, and dinner for three days. And all of a sudden, in another altered state, I had the conviction that selfishness was a problem: *I can't make myself happy this way. I need to make other people happy, too.*

Another transformative experience led to a Master's degree in Social Communication. I grew up in the forties and early fifties – a period that predated television – entirely isolated, and we didn't have radio out there except for stock market news on one station. No drugstore magazines, nothing to read, no TV, no movies – I saw my first movie when I was twelve. Then I went to the seminary and was isolated except for my intellectual studies in theology. When I came out of the seminary in the sixties to teach high school, the culture shock was just incredible. I realized these kids were completely controlled by the media so I went off and got a degree in social media.

Later on, I read a book by Adele Davis called *Let's Get Well*, and realized *Some food is good for you and some isn't, and I have to be careful.* I had thought food was like gasoline you put in your car, and I remember the transforming experience of reading the book, *Oh! It makes a difference what you eat!* All of a sudden, with the distinction between good and bad food, good and bad soil, I became seriously concerned about nutrition, a lifelong interest I maintain to this day, spending thousands of hours and dollars pursuing nutrition.

At about age 40 I got a call from my sister that she wanted me to come see her in Phoenix. My wife and I flew there, though I barely had enough money. And my friend Bill called at the same time. Also at the this time, I was being told I was going to be fired from my teaching job because I was too liberal. My sister is a remarkable woman fifteen years younger who sought me out when she was in college, and I would do anything for her. And Bill was my best friend, a big-time Eight who used to give me hell for my lack of protecting myself, scolding me for saying what I thought regardless of who was listening – from bishops to CEOs, anybody I've wanted to – because, as the Western song says, I was always "one toke over the line."

So I flew to see my sister and my best friend, arrived at 10 pm and asked my brother-in-law, who's a really good guy, "Will you take me over to see Bill tonight?" He said, "Sure, sure!" When I got there, Bill was standing underneath the street light, I gave him a big hug, and he said, "Look, we can talk later but John wants to see you. I've been building you up to him for a possible job." So I walked in at 10:30 and half an hour later agreed to take the job. The conflation of my best friend as my advocate, my sister calling me down there, and John being there – all at once – that's career planning Seven style!

That was transformative because it fit with my earlier decision to be a philosopher and theologian. And here I had a job in which I was the perfect person for the job and the job was perfect for me. It was a complete, total fit, and I flourished for 25 years. I'd work twelve hours a day if I needed to and come home refreshed. It was new ideas, it was theology, it was liberal, and it was a little bit antiauthoritarian because we were blowing the whistle on the stupid bishops all the time. Just perfect for me!

I almost lost that job six weeks after I got there. The head of the company was an easy-going Nine, and they had a really mean bastard of an Eight consultant. Everybody would go into panic mode a month before the consultant was scheduled to visit. My boss was supposed to come up with a series of things we could publish, and asked me, "Can you think of anything?" I said "Oh sure" and dashed off 20 things we could do. I knew *options*! My boss was so afraid, he loaded up on Valium and was barely conscious during the whole meeting. When the consultant attacked, my boss said I'd come up with some ideas and read off those twenty. The consultant turned to me and said sneeringly, "Well, don't *you* just go round lighting fires!" And without thinking, I said "Yeah, and you piss on them and the company runs on steam!" Everybody hated him and they burst into laughter. This Eight took me aside later and said, "You know, *you* have a personality problem. You're just too abrasive!"

He told me to take a Dale Carnegie course, the poor man's charm school. So I called up Norman Vincent Peal's outfit and said, "Send your guy out to pitch me on taking the course." The guy's first statement was, "You know, Dale Carnegie is like the bible. It's very simple and easy to understand," looking at me who had eight years of advanced scripture studies. I said, "Are you kidding? The bible is so hard to understand, the whole world is divided around it. They all think they're right and they all disagree. It's terribly complicated!" He tried again: "Oh, OK. Well, you know we're all born perfect." I said, "That's not true. Some kids are born crack babies, and with fetal alcohol syndrome!" After a few of these, he stood up and said, "I've never done this before, but I'm going to say you should not be allowed to take a Dale Carnegie course. You would ruin it; you're just too rational."

When a person is very conservative, especially religiously conservative, I will often be very funny and very mean, always combined. The kids were furious at the way I taught high school religion in the sixties because I said things like, "There's no such thing as a whale eating Jonah; this is a literary form." And I controlled them with my caustic wit. One kid at the end of the term said I should have my tongue registered as a lethal weapon. It's OK if I'm with any kind of peer, but not when I'm with Fox people. At a neighborhood barbeque this guy started going off with Republican dogma, and I made everybody laugh at him so much he left.

These altered states I've described have a spiritual component, but I don't use religious language, which is usually cultural and retro, pretentious and pompous. But the altered state *is* religious. For example, when I was in the eighth grade I had a primitive faith. I didn't live in a parish, I didn't know any priests except those who were missionaries from 40 miles away, and all but two of them spoke only German or Russian. So I grew up without any formal religious training, but I was very pious in the sense that I prayed a lot. And I thought about religious things.

There were ten kids in the family, and seven of us were valedictorians, but my oldest brother was mentally retarded. So here's this blinding contrast. We were all smart and triumphant, all successful, all athletes, my sisters were very pretty; we were genetic celebrations, and then there was my brother. I couldn't reconcile this. *Is God good or not? If He is, then why my brother's mental retardation? And if He's not, why am I so happy?* This happiness thing – I remember one day when I was in my mid-thirties, sitting up in my room and I almost spoke it out loud: *Why am I so much happier than everybody around me? I'm counseling people, helping all these high schoolers with lingering problems, and I don't have any problems. Why can I be so happy and getting all A's in school and I'm healthy and a good athlete, and then there's my brother*?

That conflict between drove me to religion. *Is God good or not?* I had to have an answer. Now I have the answer. And the answer is that I don't know. Here's the story I tell myself. Once upon a time there were twins in the womb, and one twin said to the other, "You know, I think I'll go to the other side." And the other twin said, "Oh, you're crazy! The cord's not long enough! Where would you get your food? It's nice in here! Stay here. Besides, nobody's ever come back!" And the other twin says, "I'm going to go." I think we know as much about what's on the other side as the baby in the womb. It's beyond my pay scale.

I never had a mentor until I published an Enneagram teacher's materials and then he and I talked on the telephone. I'm a very pronounced audio learner. When I hear something, I remember it. And I've learned from books. The seminary curriculum was four years of philosophy and then four years of theology. At the end of the first year of theology I was sitting on a raft on the lake with my theology teacher and he asked, "What have you been reading?" When I told him, he looked at me kind of funny and said, "Give me a list of the books you've read," so I did and I'd read 50 books outside the assigned readings. My gluttony as a Seven is not for food or sex or travel; it's for information. I still read *so* much, and I'm influenced collectively by my voracious reading habit.

I moved out to the country because of Thomas Berry's book, *The Dream of the Earth*. I live 30 miles out from the city, 15 miles from the nearest town of more than a thousand. I moved here to cultivate the earth, to be kind to the earth, to make love to the earth. I found Ken Wilber's book, *Marriage of Sense and Soul*, to be really, really wonderful. I've read it twice, and I've only read a couple of books twice. Also Walter Ong's *The Presence of the Word*. And there's a German theologian named Hans Kung. After I heard a lecture by Kung, I read a lot of his books. And of course I've read a lot about the Enneagram.

My main resistance to change has been my avoidance of hard work. I've never been able to take a job that would pay me good money if I didn't like to do it. I didn't need to hear "Do what you love." That's all I've ever done. I write easily and I write well – but it's too much work, so I don't do it much. I was involved in a project with a Nine who complained about having to do all the details and asked me to do more of them. That was a really powerful experience, and here's what happened. An Enneagram teacher had a throwaway line that really triggered me. He said, "You know, Sevens often vilify a difficult task." I thought, *Wow! I wonder if I'm doing that?* So I did something I recommend to other Sevens: Start a difficult task and then after 15 minutes ask yourself, "Is this really as painful as I had envisioned it?" I learned as I was doing that, *Hey, I really like to do this!* This told me how much I dread something when I think it's difficult, and then when I actually do it, it's not that bad at all.

It's difficult for me to maintain a consistent frame over a period of time, so the way I phrase something today I might phrase as a very different reality tomorrow. It gives me a lot of creativity but also, I might change it tomorrow. This is one reason I don't want to write it down, because I don't want to be held to "That's my opinion." The greater awareness is how I'm polarized between discipline and spontaneity. I've tended to shy away from whatever was going to require a great deal of discipline, and I've had to learn that spontaneity follows *after* discipline. I was able to be really a good debater because I had read all the books. Then I could stand up and speak freely. I'm going to a discussion group tonight, and I will be one of the few people there who has read all 800 pages of the history of John Adams. When I talk it's all about stories and jokes and laughter, but that's not what I read. I read the books with footnotes.

In the United States we tend to praise kids for being smart. Oriental cultures tend to praise kids for being diligent, for doing the struggle. I didn't have to struggle when I was growing up – all I had to do was be smart. So I always downplayed struggle, figuring it was a sign I wasn't smart enough. Consequently I would shy away from anything that would hurt my little bubble that I was smart. My Enneagram narrative was, "I'm struggling to be the smartest guy in the room." When I was younger I *was* the smartest kid in the room, and I'm still trying to be that. A number of times around here I've been introduced as "The smartest guy I know," and I think *Yeah, that sounds good. I made it!* But that's the over-identification with my ideas; very Five-ish. That's why I started talking about this polarization between discipline and spontaneity. I feared discipline because (a) it would be too hard, and (b) it would prove I'm not smart. Now when I see that pattern I think, *Oh yes, there it* is.

That's the thing I want to convey to readers. It isn't a sense of "Hey, I've arrived." I heard Richard Rohr recently, who said, "You know, I used to teach the Enneagram, and I'm a One, and what I can tell you is that I don't get angry so quickly, and when I do I'm more forgiving of myself." And I thought, *That's it! It's that simple, just being aware, seeing what's been unconscious, how it has controlled you, and being with it. Sometimes it doesn't run you, and sometimes it does.* As a Seven, of course, I use it in good humor. I started out a talk on spirituality by saying, "I've studied spirituality and I've mastered two or three traditions and I say that now I'm completely spiritually realized. My therapist says I have one little problem I need to deal with. He says I'm seriously delusional." That's it!

I pray without words. I get up in the morning, have a cup of coffee before I eat, and just sit, try not to have words. Probably my most spiritual practice is a cultivation of gratitude. I have a connection to One and the way I stop myself from being judgmental is to frequently tell myself how lucky I am. Then I don't see the problems of others as being because they're "bad." Theologians would call it *grace*.

One of my practices relates to nutrition. I've practically given up all forms of sugar, which was really hard. I usually drink my coffee black and my cereal without milk and sugar. I don't eat desserts. I don't drink much – one glass of wine four or five times a week and that's it.

I did meditate for eight years in the seminary and I gave it up because I didn't see any change in myself. Probably I also don't do meditation because it's boring. To this day I find tolerating boredom *very* difficult. I put myself in some boring situations for the sake of my wife. She will take me shopping and she's a skilled shopper – she grew up poor, too – and it takes a long time and I'm just standing there. It's really hard for me. I try to find something interesting – designer choices, or color patterns, or something – but boy it's so hard for me to remain in the present if I'm bored. Also, my observation of people who were so into meditation was sharply negative. We had a Dean of Discipline who, on Good Friday afternoon, would kneel on the tile, completely erect, for three straight hours from noon until 3:00. He was an asshole, a very rigid One with no sense of humor and he was narrow and mean and picky and nobody liked him. So all this meditation? Yeah, he did all the things a Zen master would tell him to do.

I do spiritual reading. I don't think I could get along without constantly reading about spiritual matters. I've listened to all of Eckhart Tolle's tapes and he keeps saying, "Don't identify with thought forms." Thought forms are your Enneagram style. It felt so good for me to be able to integrate that with my knowledge of the Enneagram. And of course that's how my Seven style shows up, in my cross-platform relating of things. I just listened to 48 lectures on classical music, and what I loved most was the relationship between music and spirituality and cultural patterns. For example, Bach was a Lutheran. The Catholic tradition up to that time required that music be integrated with the words because it had to be instructive. Luther said "You're saved by faith." It was the 1600's, Bach was a contemporary of Luther's and that whole Protestant reformation, so his music was his spirituality; he wrote music as a spiritual expression without words. The notion that you can reach God without words is a big part of Protestant spirituality, a big part of German mysticism, and a big part of the Protestant Reformation. And it's important to me.

Thomas Aquinas defines *chastity* as not pretending to know when you don't know. The chaste mind is so important. And for Aquinas the starting point, or *impurity*, is always in the intelligence. If you're pure in your intelligence, you don't pretend to know what you don't know. Lying, duplicity, pretense – those are the start of seduction. So that's been important, because Sevens are all about appetite. Admitting that I don't know and poking fun at myself when I pretend to know; that's been very helpful; admitting the limits of my knowledge.

Commentary

The overused gift of Style Seven is to be excited or joyful. These are ways their Egos attract attention – what's not to like about excitement or joyfulness? The two stories in this chapter illustrate what can happen when people move beyond the story their Egos are telling. Then they transform the need to be excited or joyful into something much more.

In the second story, much of Alan's "transformation has been the transformation of ideas about what is what. [...] I *really* live in my head!" In Jessica's story, it's about things becoming different, "it's not like the old disappears, but it's unrecognizable." In these accounts, as ideas, perspectives and notions transform, Ego's control relaxes and more of their innate wisdom can emerge.

A common trait of people of Style Seven is to blend out that which is unpleasant or doesn't fit their Ego's program of striving to be excited or joyful. For Jessica, the process of nudging out of the comfort zone began when she moved from Southern California to Minnesota to attend college and began interacting with people who did not share similar experiences of life. (Yes, Minnesota also has a Cambridge!) Her story charts how the good-looking façade carefully constructed by Ego began to lose its luster as more and more experiences helped to relax Ego's grip.

In moments when Ego relaxes, a person of Style Seven can experience the virtue of *Sobriety*, which Jerry Wagner describes as "staying in the present and living a balanced life, taking in only as much as you need, and expending only as much energy as is called for." This description points to a better connection to reality rather than the highs that come with striving to be excited. We see this when one of Jessica's professors confronted her about her family of origin, which led her into therapy and into working the Twelve Steps of Al-Anon. This is where she began to confront her fears about what would happen when her defense mechanism, her pretending that everything's ok, would fall apart.

In the second story, the strategy of Alan's Ego to find excitement and joy was to coast. His first "D" in college led to the realization that he might have to *work* to get through school. Again and again, Alan receives reminders from life that there is an alternative to coasting. An alternative that leads to a deeper and richer life in which he experiences the higher quality of *Wisdom*. He describes this as "Now I have the answer. And the answer is I don't know." Not knowing is also something he holds lightly, evidenced by how he opened a talk on spirituality, "I've studied spirituality and I've mastered two or three traditions and I say that now I'm completely spiritually realized. My therapist says I have one little problem I need to deal with. He says I'm seriously delusional."

Thought forms are integral to Alan's Enneagram Style. So, when he was listening to his Eckhard Tolle tapes, the statement "Don't identify with thought forms" resonated strongly. This has led him to draw inspiration from the music of Bach, a form of spiritual expression without words.

Today, both Alan and Jessica describe in similar ways how they move beyond the stories their Egos are telling. In Alan's case, it is to stay with difficult tasks. Instead of vilifying these tasks, he has adopted the practice of working for 15 minutes on a task and then asking himself if this was as painful as he had envisioned. Jessica's way is to stay with the difficult moments in life and learn from them, to recognize "I see the world not as it is but as I am." Her work around healing the Heart center and allowing its intended purpose has facilitated the shift from intellectual to intimate relationships with people, in the full knowledge that this leaves her open. As Jessica closes her story, "it's when hearts break that they start to expand."

Three questions to ponder:

- What happens when I stay in a difficult moment and don't walk away?

- How can I accept my progress and let go of my need for perfection?

- How do I recognize my innate wisdom speaking?

Contents

1. Gathering Courage – Ursula's story   123

2. Out of the Box – Jeff's Story   127

3. Commentary   133

Chapter Eight – Style Eight

Gathering Courage – Ursula's story

I can remember the exact date of what was probably my last big transformational experience. It was absolutely incredible, gut-wrenching! As if I had shed my skin! I recognized I could no longer live the way I had been living with the man I was married to for twelve years. It was a lie, it was unauthentic, it was so incongruent with who I was and what I believed. It had been impossible to sort out what was me and what was my own internalization of other peoples' expectations. It wasn't a conscious notion that I was setting aside my *self*. I didn't say, *Well, this is what they expect so this is what I'll do, even though I don't want to*. But when this shift occurred, those others' voices were totally eliminated. Their *shoulds* and their rules for my life were blown out of the water. Gone. Totally invalid. And it scared the fucking shit out of me! It was terrifying and yet I've got to tell you, somewhere in there was exhilaration.

This is transformation – profound moments in my life, actual events where I came out the other side.

I remember standing in the shower with my friend at the Y, buck naked, sixteen years old. She asked me, "What do you really wish for?" And I said, "You know what, I just hope my life isn't too easy." I guess I was thinking, *I want to wrestle, I want to engage, I want it to be full, I want it to be real, I don't want it to be all warm and fuzzy, I want to really live*. I once participated in a native American ceremony where I was given the name, "She who farts like a bear." That's where I am – I want to be who I am without apology! I also want to be able to acknowledge my own shit and I don't want to have to hide it from others, but sometimes I'm less successful than others – it's part of my history to hide it from myself. You know, I really did think I was doing the right thing. From childhood right on through, I thought I was attempting to live a good life. But it was a delusion. This can be bad if I'm being hyper-responsible – which I tend to do – because then I'm the fixer, I'll take care of it. And tied to this willingness to acknowledge my own shit is the tendency to go too far, taking on too much, and then that becomes a burden.

I feel like I'm moving now. I'm going through some changes and my husband is seeing me as a different person. He's sometimes baffled, I think, uncomfortable. And here's a paradox: I'm baffled, too, except I'm moving into this new place of comfort that feels real, like I'm getting down to the core.

I had been estranged from my parents for three years. When I divorced my first husband to marry my second husband my mother stopped speaking to me, and my father followed suit. Then I found out through my son that my dad had a heart attack. When my son called, there was another shift from, *Well, OK, this is the way they want it*, to *Fuck what they want! I'm done! I'm not playing by their rules. I'm not doing this anymore*! I went home, called immediately, and we were there that day. Well, she was a bitch with a capital B for months. It finally warmed up, and relations – as they say – have normalized. But here's the way I'm different. Before, she never hugged me, I wouldn't hug her. She wouldn't tell me she loved me, I'd never tell her I loved her. Her rules. *This is the way she wants it, OK, I respect that.* Now that's over: I hug her, I touch her, I tell her I love her. And you know what's happened? She's changed. This last time when my husband and I went on vacation and they were nearby, she could not keep her hands off of me. And it was real! When we left, I remember especially she just held my arms and looked right at me. Isn't that amazing! I talked to her on the phone last night, and at the end I said, "I love you." And she said, "Oh, I love you, too." There you go! That's how I've changed. And look what happened!

I've always had people who've helped me along the way. In my childhood my Dad was a great dad for a little kid – playful, active, doing cartwheels, handstands, very physical, fun and funny, and then I got to be fourteen and whoa! I got turned over to my mother, and we know what that was like! I remember in my teens telling my mother I really felt I was falling apart and she said, "Well, now I suppose you're going to tell me you need a psychiatrist!" You know what I did? I said, "I don't need anything," and shut it all down, and it was gone. But I had a surrogate family, the family of my best friend – who's still my best friend in the whole world. I lived with her family and they loved me unconditionally – they thought I was absolutely terrific! People who challenge you can be resources, too. My so-called ex-husband was the ultimate challenge in that he was perfect for all my buried shit. Perfect!

Chapter Eight

I was raised to marry him with the messages, *Make everything OK for everybody else. Don't have a feeling of your own.* It was brutal.

I've had little success with therapists – perhaps because I wasn't ready, perhaps because the right "teacher" didn't appear, most likely because I'd bought the message *I don't need anything* to the point of *It's not OK for me to get help*. I did finally find help with one psychologist, but before that it was just an intellectual exercise.

I go on long walks and my preparation beforehand is, *I'm not going to think about anything and I'm going to think about everything! Whatever I draw to me, I'll take it in*. It was on one of these walks that I had an encounter with a Red Fox. It was just incredible, man, truly awesome! I was leaving a meadow heading into the woods, and being open. There before me was this creature, just a few feet away, and I thought, *Is that a dog? Oh, fuck! It's a red fox!* This is really hard to put into words, but we just looked at each other for an endless amount of time and there was no fear. Then as soon as I became self-conscious, she looked at me and turned and walked away – didn't run, walked away, at the moment I became self-conscious. *Did I make this up? I don't even care*! But it was absolutely a going down.

That same kind of opening, that same receptive state I use on these walks, I also use in my meditation. I see steps made of stone that take me into a pool in which I submerge myself, and then I go farther down through what looks like a storm sewer, but I end up in a place where I'm floating or flying. And that's an energizing piece of this, because that little seed or acorn or whatever comes out, goes above me, catches all the energy that's in the universe then goes back into me. In the next stage there's a vortex. I go down into this vortex and there's a person there, real androgynous. His name is Paul. Boy this sounds crazy! This is anonymous, right? Well, he is constantly there – he, she, it – he is constantly there and we have dialogue. He never, ever, ever, ever tells me what to do. He just asks the right questions. Sometimes we sit by a fire and talk and then sometimes I go into his cabin and rest. In the final place is a sea that's similar to the one in *Journey to the Center of the Earth*. And it's down in the guts because I go into the sea and look up and I can see a heart beating, pulsing.

I've kept a diary since I was ten years old. And drawing. As a child, even, I'd go up to my room, close my door, lock it, get my pencils and paper out, and draw scenes. The other thing I've always done is get into my body: walk, run, feel the burn, treadmill, swimming, those kinds of things. I like a book called *Sweat Your Prayers*.

If I feel threatened I withdraw. Maybe it's the Eight disintegrating to Five, but there are times in my marriage where we will have a disagreement and I get angry, then I get hurt, then I go away. It's not conscious; I don't say to myself, *I'm going to withdraw.* I fucking disintegrate! That's what it feels like! My thoughts are gone, I'm in little pieces, feeling, *That's enough, go away, stop, I am gone, I am out of here.* So I don't want to paint myself as some paragon. Heaven forbid! When I feel defensive – when I'm trying to defend my ego – I get in my own way. This occurs when I feel attacked by someone really important to me. You know, there are other people who can attack me and I'll turn it right back on them, or let them know how little their opinion means to me. But when I'm self-conscious, conscious of how I might be harmed, that's when the armor goes up. It doesn't let anything out and it doesn't let anything in.

Do you know the book, *The Soul's Code*, by James Hillman? The premise is that you come into the world with a soul, a core that's solid, real, warm, and all this light resonates from it. What appeals to me about this metaphor is that oftentimes when we think about spirituality it's kind of a coming up and going out. This is not. This is going in and going down, and that really resonates with me. I'm being drawn down, and yet it's not ever a place I'll reach because it's never-ending. The other thing I know is that it's always been there. It's always been with me.

The only advice for other Eights that comes to mind is something I think is pretty commonly known. And that would be, *When you're in it, stay in it. Don't push it away. Don't leave. Stay there. You may find it's not what you thought it might be.* I was working with my therapist on a dream where I was running away from something, really terrified. I remember running down this hall, and behind me these monsters – creepy-crawly things – were after me. And I got to this door thinking, *Don't open the door! Don't open the door! Oh, God, don't open the door! What if these creatures come and they open the door?* I opened the door, and you know what was there? It was a little Jack-in-the-Box. It came out and went *Boinggg*, and I said, *You're kidding!* It had a really ugly face, but I was like, *And...?* So that's what I mean, don't waste your energy wrestling things to the ground, because you may not need to. Stay with it. And just have courage.

Chapter Eight

Out of the Box – Jeff's Story

I think of *transformation* as opening a door I've never opened. And in many cases it's a door I've seen and wondered about, but I was either afraid or simply unable to approach the door or open it. And suddenly a whole new place has opened up that you can walk into and look around and see how wholly different it is from where you were, where the possibilities are endless.

I have a long history of seeking peak experiences, seeking adrenaline rushes, climbing rocks, hanging from one hand over precipices and things like that. I was always keen on river rafting and I wanted to do it in wild rivers like the Amazon: rivers you could gauge by the number of maimings they have per season. There's probably nothing more exhilarating than going down a rapids with nothing but a helmet and a jacket and a life vest. And kicking yourself off of rocks as they come to you, and trying to keep your head up far enough where you can see them and presenting either your feet or a shoulder to something you're going to hit so you aren't simply splatted like a fly swatter! That's a kick. Last year I was hit by a truck, and badly broke some ribs and an arm – with some nerve damage. It was distressing from the point of view that I'm not the same person I once was, now being only as strong as a regular person.

My wife and I were sitting in front of our therapist when he said a few simple words that opened a door. It was very much like the movie, *What Dreams May Come*, where Robin Williams dies and everything is sort of Technicolor. There I was in this place that was different from where I just left. I was loaded with feelings and thoughts about what's possible from this new place inside the door, instead of standing outside looking at it. The therapist had asked, "What do you feel like when you see your wife depressed or unhappy?" and I had at first answered with, "Helpless in the face of her discomfort." And he wasn't buying that. He said, "I would have expected you to say something like, 'I see how badly you feel. Is it anything I am doing, or is there anything I can do about it?'" And I thought, *My God! Such a simple statement, so easily made, so totally different than anything I would have ever thought of!* If I can simply make statements like that in the face of my wife's distress, it's a whole new place to be! It wasn't much, but it was a lot for me. I realized I had grown up in a place where when you're hurt or in pain you go away alone and come back out when you're healed. What I learned simply wasn't the right stuff – it thwarted my growth in the area of caring for people and being cared for, in ways I never would have suspected. To me, that was a transforming moment.

Being hit by a truck forced me to ask for help in ways I never had before. I had always tended to be at sixes and sevens when it came to, on the one hand, having the most qualified person do it, and on the other hand, doing everything myself, approaching every act as a Warrior with absolutely everything he's got. It's a guaranteed burn-out, but that's one of the facts of life for Warriors. This was deeply frustrating because you can't do everything. My sense of failure was always with me because I put myself in a no-win. So the experience of being partially incapacitated gave me the feeling I can say no sometimes to things in a way I couldn't have before. I haven't gotten perfect at that yet – the habit of doing everything is still with me. It's one of the constant challenges I face, but I'm getting better because the awareness is there that I'm not as strong as I was. That also means I'm not as dumb as I was and I don't have to do all this stuff and I don't have to pretend I can. So I recognized a physical difference but there was an emotional change, too, of facing reality. I mean, what becomes the credibility of somebody who doesn't perform like he says he will, both to himself and to the people around him?

Like anybody who's over 50 – or 40, or 30, I've had a lot of encounters with people, both superficial and more profound, and the person I brought to them was not a person who could really enrich them or their lives. I'm sure a lot of people saw good stuff in me, but I wasn't able to bring all I could to them because I was far too insular. And I often think of the loss, both to me and to all those people, of what could have been. I was ignorant as a post, simply not equipped to talk about larger issues – my ability to hear was incapacitated.

Now I'd say I'm more participative, somehow. What I mean by that is *being* with somebody when I'm with them, actually sharing what's going on, rather than standing at something of a distance and pot-shooting at what they're saying. Yeah, and I'm self-disclosing with more ease, and on subjects I never dreamed of talking to anyone else about. Before, I was always back there in the cave, conjecturing, and I would never share. When I'm really listening to someone now, it's like walking down the sidewalk with our arms around each other, in step, making eye contact, walking together. To me it's nothing more and nothing less than being with someone, right with them. I remember, when Dad died, how awful I felt leaving his bedside with him not having enough strength to open his eyes but being conscious behind his lids, and his life draining away. And I thought to myself that I was truly alive in my grief for him, in my sense of who he was. To me, that was a good outcome of his dying, that all the clutter that can keep me from being in the moment went away.

My wife has been a support in voicing what I struggle with: An amazing number of times I'll be in the awareness *I don't have to...* or *I shouldn't agree to take this on...* and my wife will say exactly what I'm thinking and it will tip me toward taking an appropriate position. My tendency is to try to bunch things together in a way that creates an impossible set of circumstances, and her efforts are to spread out what I do to actually occupy times when they can realistically be done. I might still say, *Nahhh...* but the unreality of the position I've taken will gnaw at me in ways that would never have touched me before.

I don't believe there's any guiding higher power, or any natural urge toward positive direction. I do believe there are laws governing us that, if you were to list them, would become the characteristics of that higher power. For example, there's a law that's built into our humanness of a need for connectedness that's similar to gravity. These are natural laws. We can operate in concert with them or fight them, but if we had a list of these laws and acted in concert with them, I'm hesitant to say what would ever form our limits as sentient souls. Somehow, I do believe in the soul, in the essence of us. I can't say it lives beyond our death, but I get glimpses from another dimension that I don't feel compelled to understand. In each of these moments we're going through, we have choices of *What is the law that's prevailing at this moment, and am I in concert with it or am I fighting it?*

For me it's being in touch with the real, being in touch with the same things I was in touch with when Dad died. Moments when everything falls away, where – without distraction – you can be wholly where you are and in touch with all that's good. There's an experience – when I'm drawing or painting or just looking around me – where I see something that's the absolute, total epitome of what it is: it's a tree that is the perfect sycamore, it's a child's drawing, or someone looking at someone else lovingly. That's what *poignancy* means for me. What gives meaning to my life is seeing people, not necessarily at their best, but in the wholeness of who they are, unfettered by fears or distractions.

I don't deal in images much. But when the therapist gave me that piece of paper with four or five points of what to do, step-by-step, to get in contact with my feelings so I could speak from my feelings, that did touch me as a path to communication I don't exercise but is available to me. This was very similar to what I felt when he said, "What if you tried this?" in listening to my wife, and I thought, *Oh, there's something I can do.*

I was a long time letting go of the notion that two people of intelligence and good will can find a way through a problem without outside help. And even though I'd been through the Forum, where the concept of the "box" was brought home to me, I never really applied it to myself, that there are things you just can't see because you're inside the box. My world would have been a different place if I'd understood earlier that someone else could help me. It's another facet of my insularity. And of course, when it comes down finally to it, it's not a matter of skills, it's not a matter of adroitness, it's not a matter of sensitivity, it's a matter of being inside the box.

My lack of self-disclosure and tendency to stereotype people are barriers to change. People may have said something to me, but I just couldn't hear it. What was lacking in me was *empathy*. It's a trite word, *listening*, but I just never did it before! And part of listening was responding to make sure I heard what they said, and I didn't do that. I can think of at least two women I lost because I wasn't open enough. The first one knew my feelings were strong and I was dedicated to her, but thought I was just too wild a child to be dependable. And that was exacerbated, I'm sure, by my tending towards an insularity that didn't give her a lot to hold onto. The loss of the second woman was much the same thing, actually. I cared for her a lot, she knew that, and I was long past being a wild child, but I was still insular and not sharing or collaborative, so she went away. I think in her heart, finally, what bothered her most was that she didn't feel I needed anybody.

I've also tended to put people in a box, hear some words, and say to myself, *Oh, there they go again* and act out of that assumption as opposed to where they really are. *Categorize them as soon as possible so you can put them away and let them just rattle on, and mentally go about your own business.* A horrid place, as much for oneself as well as for them, because if you're not there you're not in real time, you're not

Chapter Eight

in the moment. And in truth, you're not anyplace. You're mentally staring off into space and giving up the opportunity to live.

I see it *as stepping out of the box*: We spend most of our lives exploring the corners of our box. Then when we step out of it into a new, larger box it becomes the object of the remaining lifetime to explore the corners and pieces of that box. That's what I'm doing and that's what I think the *path* is, learning what life is all about inside this box. There's an endless supply of boxes, each one containing new wisdom, new insights. As you're stepping across into the next larger box, you are at that moment the epitome of the old box, you are all that the old box can be, you've taken all that it can give you. And then it's time for the new box. It's not only being able to look over the fence and see into the old box, but having genuinely new stuff that wasn't visible to you from being inside the walls of the old box. And by and large, you've got to have help to see outside of it. You're in the box, and either you open the door or somebody else opens the door, and on the other side you're in this Technicolor place, a place where you can't, you mustn't stop listening.

I tell myself *Listen to everything, make it important: be present and don't characterize. Don't necessarily do anything, but really be there while you're talking, while you're doing things together, and let that lead to whatever changes come down the pike.* I want to become aware, in a deeper way, of what I want from my life. I think of that wonderful story Mel Brooks told about Moses coming down from the mountain with two tablets and standing before the multitude, stepping up on a rock, losing his balance. As he was saying, "I've got to share with you the twenty..." one tablet fell and broke, and he finished, "...ten commandments!" There are other things equally important to traditional values that are on the broken tablet – like anger – that don't appear in the ten commandments, but are as life-damaging as any other of the more heinous things you could give in to.

In terms of my own criteria for life, my primary one is illustrated by the story of the ten *talents* from the bible. The father gave his three sons ten *talents* each and set them adrift, and they all came back. One of them gambled it away, another invested it but lost it, and the third one buried his – so he still had ten *talents*. The father took back the first two sons and divided his kingdom among them, but he told the third son to take his goddamn ten *talents* and shove them up his ass! That was what the son was given to make his life from, and all he had at the end was what he started with. So the others may have lost, but at least they risked. And every moment is a *talent*.

Chapter Eight

Commentary

The overused gift of Style Eight is to be powerful. It is their Ego's way of attracting attention. And theirs is a great gift: who can be powerful is really somebody! The two stories in this chapter illustrate what can happen when people move beyond the story their Egos are telling. When they transform the need to be powerful into something much more.

In these stories, transformation is no one-off event. It is a sequence of "profound moments in my life, actual events where I came out the other side," as Ursula puts it. Indeed, one of these moments is likened to shedding skin. For Jeff transformation is likened to "opening a door I've never opened." Each one of these profound moments is a milestone on the journey from somebody to nobody. They illustrate how these moments help to relax the Ego's control, so that more of the innate can emerge in their lives.

A common trait of people of Style Eight is to not admit to needing help, to say "I don't need anything." This is part of Ego's story of striving to be powerful, to be in control. In Ursula's story, her experience of relaxing Ego came through experiencing unconditional love from the family of her best friend. She charts the deepening experiences of relaxing the Ego throughout her life.

In moments when the Ego relaxes, a person of Style Eight can experience the virtue of *Innocence*, which Jerry Wagner describes as "love expressed as a childlike response to the present moment." We see this recalled poetically in Ursula's encounter with the Red Fox, where she experienced true connection – until she became self-conscious (Ego no longer relaxed). Another common thread in this story is how quickly "the armor goes up" when she's self-conscious: "It doesn't let anything out and it doesn't let anything in."

In Jeff's story, he describes his Ego armor in terms of being too insular, in a lack of self-disclosure. The story charts the profound moments that helped to weaken this insularity, moments where he's in touch with the real. This story provides beautiful examples of how, when Ego is relaxed, a person of Style Eight can experience the higher quality of *Truth*, which he describes as "seeing people, not necessarily at their best, but in the wholeness of who they are, unfettered by fears or distractions."

The more Jeff does this, the deeper becomes his experience of life. He describes it as a process of stepping out of a box into a larger box, exploring this in all its Technicolor glory and then finding it opens into an even larger box. Again and again. Key in this process has been the dawning realization that it's OK – even necessary – to allow others to help him move into the larger box.

Today, they describe in very similar ways how they get beyond the story their Ego is telling. For Ursula it's *"When you're in it, stay in it. Don't push it away. Don't leave. Stay there. You may find it's not what you thought it might be."* To be present in the moment and see what unfolds and how it unfolds. To allow it to take the shape it takes. For Jeff it's presence through true listening: *"Listen to everything, make it important: be present and don't characterize. Don't necessarily do anything, but really be there while you're talking, while you're doing things together, and let that lead to whatever changes come down the pike."* Both descriptions illustrate the power of transformation in a person of Style Eight.

Three questions to ponder:

- What is the nature of my armor that keeps me in and others out?

- Which door do I need to open next and who can help me?

- When did I last express a childlike response to the present moment?

Contents

1. Boxes and Spheres Moving Through Time – Claire's story   137

2. Two Steps Forward, One Step Back – Ralph's Story   144

3. Commentary   150

Chapter Nine – Style Nine

Boxes and Spheres Moving Through Time – Claire's story

The word *transformation* definitely has a positive meaning for me. Also sometimes I think of it as *shifting*. I picture moving to the side to go forward in a different way, a *shift* rather than a *drift*, a sense of coming into closer alignment with deep values I haven't always acted on. So *transforming* would be aligning myself more with an underlying theme that feels most genuine in my life.

The first transforming experience that comes to mind was in high school, being in a wilderness camp setting for five weeks, working with a dozen other people in an unfamiliar setting and recognizing my contribution to life in a different way – a sense of humor, a more adventurous, whimsical side – and also the importance of connection to others, learning about different people, being present with them in that moment. That was a peak experience for me, just one example of other times where a group was formed ahead of time and then created an identity, but also sometimes where I've actually helped such a small group come about, where there's real connection. That wasn't my earliest experience of some sort of shift, but it was a very powerful experience. Though there was some sorrow as we left the group, it has continued to bear very rich fruit through the years, and has been a touchstone for other kinds of events that were nourishing to me or where I found I had been nourishing to others.

At the time I wasn't thinking in terms of an Enneagram framework. But when I came to the Enneagram in the last decade as a very rich and true way of viewing things, it resonated with patterns I've had all my life. I don't remember them in infancy or elementary school, but by high school certain patterns of responding to the world were definitely there that I now characterize as being typically Nine-like. Not being immediately certain of what I feel, having to come around to it indirectly and sometimes by hearing other people speak and seeing if I agree with them or not. Some hesitancy in taking a stand or going with a particular choice, whether for my own actions or in helping other people decide what to do. I've been someone to observe and fit in rather than take a definitive direction, until afterwards when I might feel regret about not having done something. A tendency to fall asleep to the things most important to me, to go along, to drift, to be very busy and do a lot of things but not do the most important things, and only realize that afterwards because I wasn't being present.

I think of the word *inertia* in a physics way; it doesn't mean you're standing still – you're going somewhere but without taking any actions to change your direction or velocity. So the difficult side for me as a Nine is being in that state of inertia, doing something or not doing something. Occasionally something kicks me out of it, something that's so inspiring it can't be ignored. And it's very easy at that point. It's not work, it just happens. When I came home from the wilderness camp, I was changed in being able to see the world differently.

Certainly the aspect of understanding our own patterns and recognizing them in a nonjudgmental way is true for any Enneagram style. I think a shift may come for some people with a different language. For me there's something very powerful about metaphorical storytelling. The parables and the language of poetry are strong themes in my life, very inspiring. That's the way I learn things most powerfully and the way I express things with most meaning. Even though my job wouldn't typically be thought of as that kind of work, it's still the way I'm most effective in reaching other people. As a physician my logical, fact-based approach, skills, and technical experience are all very important as a useful frame of reference, but the extent to which I bring what energizes me personally into my workplace and family life is probably healthier.

The experience of coaching this past year has been very helpful. I've become more explicit about how I can be present with myself in a supportive way, even when things are difficult. I'm seeing any discomfort I feel as just as interesting and important to follow as when I feel happy and excited. Whether something is drawing me in a positive way or repelling me, I follow those signals instead of putting them away. If my immediate response to someone's proposal is negative, or I do not like someone's personality trait, I now know there's something there to teach me. I used to bury my reaction or try to ignore it. Now I see it as a real gift to notice the humor in something, or to see an opportunity in what at first feels like a problem and turn it into something that can be managed or find a new direction.

For instance, I've gone deeper into understanding my particular faith path, which for me is a progressive Christian path, finding I can be open to other spiritual beliefs and feel they're equally valid, yet still know the specific path I'm on is right for me, not one to reject in favor of a potpourri of things from different faiths that may seem appealing on the surface. I've matured into getting to the core of things and not being threatened by other pathways. I'm not threatened by a different belief about something. I'm interested in learning about it, clarifying further how I understand things, and I don't lose integrity. Sometimes it changes how I understand things, in a good way, and sometimes it doesn't, but it helps to learn more about it. In my family growing up, there was active discussion about different kinds of beliefs within the overall Christian tradition, so it wasn't a very fundamentalist approach, but I rarely took the opportunity – either in writing or in conversation – to actually speak to my beliefs. Perhaps I understood them but they were a conglomeration of different traditions and snatches of hymns, some sort of not-conscious framework. Maybe then I felt I had to set up artificial boundaries in order to clarify for myself where my beliefs started and stopped. But now, as I've come gradually to feel more comfortable expressing what is most meaningful to me, it's easier to listen to different points of view, to be truly interested, without being threatened. In retrospect, I think that comes from being more articulate about myself and my own journey; seeing more clearly the impact of my faith on my actions in daily living.

I'm also different in playing more and having more of a sense of humor about things I think will be difficulties throughout my life; rather than being angry and frustrated or treating them as black or white, good or bad. An example would be how I tend to let papers collect, postponing things so over time boxes of items collect that might be treasures or might be unfinished business or things I should have thrown away. That's an ongoing piece of work, to not put things in boxes but to handle them at the time and keep them in the light until they're managed. But I can also have a sense of humor about the fact that I do put things in physical boxes. It's just the way I am. Not to the extent of being a hoarder, but to the extent of having things around that don't need to be, that could have been handled simply when they first came to me, but got postponed, and now are just kind of hanging on me. The way it's shifted is not that I don't do it anymore, because that's just my default tendency, but having a bit more of a sense of playfulness and seeing some fun in actually opening up those Pandora's boxes, dealing with them and giving myself some concrete wins; taking it down to little pieces. So rather than thinking *I have twenty boxes*, I think *Well, I could just take this small square foot area and make sure that's taken care of.* Chunking down things that seem unmanageable and saying, *"Yeah, I can do this; I can do this part of it.* Whether it's a physical box or a little box to take off a checklist, I can approach things more positively by being less all-or-nothing about it, and over time I've become more patient with myself about working with my difficulties, rather than beating myself up about them.

Seeing both parents and parents-in-law pass has been transforming, those precious last days and minutes of life I've been able to spend with them. Likewise, seeing my children grow up, the moments of understanding that came even before they could speak – that connection was so strong and that sense of being in harmony. So those were touch points from which I can view some of the more mundane parts of daily living and see how present I would like to be as much of my time as possible. Your relationship is deeper when you know you won't have someone with you forever and you act on it. My mother had Alzheimer's, yet was still very present in her last days and our relationship was equally deep, in a unique way I would not have appreciated even a few months before – when I'd been focused on her disabilities and my lack of ability to communicate. Then I realized I was trying too hard, and a different kind of communication occurred that was very lucid and very real, when I gave myself permission to spend time with her rather than just managing her affairs and feeding her intermittently. To be in some sort of flow with her, even in that sad time, was very joyful. It's a joy you don't expect because it's not happy; it's joyful in a deep sense, feeling *This moment matters, this relationship matters and it's OK even though it's very sad.*

To help myself stay present, I need to be outdoors and engaged in some way in the natural world. I used to take this for granted and now realize how important and nourishing it is – taking walks, hiking, walking meditation. Also small group discussions, often centered around a particular book or topic, that might last for a period of a few months or a year, where I get to know people well in relation to a topic we all care about, and take specific actions between meetings. Or a group that's embarked on a trip; that kind of framework where a small group of people gather together around a particular area of interest but we're doing something actively in relation to that, not just sitting around talking philosophically, but grounding us in something we all support each other in doing. The practicing part doesn't always come automatically to me, so I try to build it in, make time for these groups in my life, which makes it easier to keep things real and not get too diffuse.

Reading definitely helps. I love word play, not just poetry but powerful novels and eloquent essays that make me see things freshly. The challenge, particularly in these days of the Internet, is that one thing can easily bridge to another. It's very exciting for me to make all those links but also more challenging to be sure at the end of an hour I remember what I was doing or what was really interesting about what I found. Otherwise, I forget it.

Certainly coaching has been helpful, in terms of reflecting back what I'm thinking, helping me articulate my thoughts more clearly. And the counselor from the camp experience I mentioned, definitely teachers, even back to one particular elementary school teacher who became a friend later in life when I was babysitting her kids and got to know her in a different way. Growing up I loved babysitting because I'd go to someone else's house and, without spying, be able to see another way of living, another set of relationships and be invited into them in a certain way. Even though I was shy and quiet with their parents, I was beloved by the little ones. I got along with them well and had patience and ideas of what to do. Some of those families also became people I could see modeling parts of my life after, adults I admired when I was growing up. And again, there was something about being in an unusual setting, different people, different things on the wall stimulating my imagination – it was so much fun and then I got paid for it!

I've also had wonderful mentors throughout my medical career who have been very skilled at what they do and also very loving and visionary. I could also appreciate, in their framework for their work, the essence of what I'd like to be. Receiving Christmas cards from these people who helped me earlier in my career and still care about me is very moving, and makes me want to be that person more for other people.

I get in my own way sometimes when I don't articulate things clearly. If there's an idea I've expressed and someone else has expressed it more clearly and concretely, everyone runs with that other person's statements and I think, *Well, didn't I just say that?* But I realize it's not because they were trying to exclude me but because they didn't hear it coming from me in a very distinctive way, and it may have taken that other person to translate it more obviously. Oftentimes when I don't make the effort to articulate something, and then it happens despite my inaction, I'll think, *Well, I could have done that,* but in fact I didn't do it. It's not about getting credit, it's about wanting to contribute and feeling I could have contributed more if I had jumped in when I wasn't completely sure of all twenty elements, when I only knew ten of them. I haven't wanted to speak up until I'm sure, but sometimes the moment is gone when it would have been useful! My take-home message is to try to express myself clearly and not worry about the outcomes. Doing something less fully baked sooner is important, to start something rather than wait until it's perfect, to get a nugget out there that people can work with, rather than holding back until it's ready to be put out on the street.

There's a gap between the poetic statement I might have that empowers me and getting something down – the three-to-five bullet approach. I haven't boiled things down when thinking, *Gotta address everything, gotta go further.* It's important to keep myself accountable to do things I want to do, because otherwise I become very *floaty*. Even if it's a good kind of dreaminess, things aren't getting done that really need to get done and then I start to feel pressed because something's due or I've been ignoring some big, practical action.

Knowing about the Nine's anger has been a helpful part of the Enneagram for me, realizing I've tamped down anger. I now recognize better when I'm ignoring it, thinking I don't feel angry and then surprising people around me when it comes out in an inappropriately strong fashion – where the situation I'm responding to in no way deserves that kind of reaction, when I didn't express any of the last nine aspects of it, so it all had to be put into the tenth time, and everybody's kind of taken aback by it, including me. I'm now more aware earlier on, thinking about why I might feel angry over something, so I can express it in a more nuanced way or more realistic to the situation. And I've come to understand that *peace* is not just the absence of tension. It's OK to have tension, to dislike something, and manage it in a way that leads to deeper harmony. Things are not always right, they're not always peaceful, nor do I have to feel great peace about everything. Emotions that come up might be there for a good reason, and ignoring them is not, in the end, going to make them go away.

A *boxes* metaphor is strong for me this year. When I used to visualize where I was, I'd see my different roles on a page, but now I'm making that schematic framing of my different roles in life more playful, more positive, more three-dimensional, more enlivening, visualizing boxes and spheres moving through time. In the visual my forearms are parallel to the ground and elbows at my side, my hands cupped and open like you might cup your hands to get well water or to hold something you're treasuring in your hands. Sometimes I visualize being open to anything; other times I picture bouncing these aspects of my life in this cupped area. Holding my hands this way is a metaphor for how I want to be in life.

Two Steps Forward, One Step Back – Ralph's Story

I had to be quite late in life to experience what I think of as *transformation*. Even though I've been in the public limelight for a very long time and had no problems as a professor in a research-oriented university, a great deal of shyness controlled my personal life until I was in my early fifties. Professorially, I could give a lecture; but on a personal basis, whether seeking directions or making a reservation at a restaurant or calling for a taxi, I would avoid having to ask for something.

It was a hostage situation where I held *myself* hostage. We would not be having this conversation even 15 years ago, because I would have been inhibited; I just couldn't have executed calling you. By my late forties I was so tired of isolating myself I started doing something about it, and this began to transform me into someone who now can ask for what I want. Still, the first thought that comes into my consciousness is *This doesn't sound like a good idea*. But I can do it.

It continues to be true for me that if I walk into a room and the signals I get from the first person I contact aren't signals that make me feel comfortable, it's predictable that I will instantly go into a shut down, withdrawn state. I have a little conversation with myself and, from a cognitive, rational point of view, there isn't a lot of evidence that I won't be able to put myself out there, but that doesn't help the emotional state that comes over me. And it goes really fast past the point of no return. I was at a party recently where I knew no one except the couple that brought me. It was a fairly high-level group of people, and on the way I obsessed about how this party was going to go. It could have been very real that I would have not enjoyed myself if I'd had initial contact with someone who made me feel "less than." That's been my experience forever. It's frustrating.

In my role as professor I was very comfortable giving a lecture, unless it involved presenting what I personally had been doing, in which case my mind immediately went to *What are they going to think about me*? Then I would become very self-conscious. It's very much linked to decisions. *What happens if they ask me a question and I have to make a decision?*

Chapter Nine

I'm not sure how I got myself to make these changes, just a feeling of *I can't stand this anymore; I have to do something*. At that time I was beginning to study about intuition, going on the presumption that I did not have intuition. I started reading a book by Shakti Gawain and asked a therapist friend about intuition. I wondered whether my inability to ask for something was because I was in such a pragmatic world that either I shouldn't be asking for it or if I did what would I answer if they asked a question? I was so convinced I didn't have intuition and I knew people who seemed to be intuitive, so it was basically discovering it. So maybe that was the door for me. Within two years of that a friend introduced me to the Enneagram, which resonated with me. Then I had the opportunity to take some weekend workshops with Helen Palmer in the city where I lived.

I first learned the Enneagram types as our defense mechanisms. I'm not saying that's the way they are *now* to me, but that's the way I learned them. And because I have a good sense of being judgmental, I immediately gravitated to the negative side of *What are the defense mechanisms?* as opposed to the positives that can come out of that philosophy. I wasn't sure I was a Nine until after I'd taken a few workshops and had been in a couple of different groups, then realized I wasn't comfortable until I was in a Nine group.

For me, judging was one of my curses forever. I would always be comfortable in a conversation – with people I knew or didn't know – if it tended toward criticism. And criticism has a tinge of judgmentalness to it. It's a cheap form of conversation. I bet two Nines could discuss what we *don't* like and not run out of time. It's very seductive to stay in the negative, because it flows. I try to catch myself joining in criticism and stop, so I don't do that much anymore.

This came from a couple of role models. When I started this journey on awareness and intuition, I noticed that two colleagues at the university where I was teaching just didn't have anything negative to say; they always spoke from a positive place. Then I challenged myself, *Could I do that? Could I even go a day without saying something negative, or a few hours, and not think from the position of the negative*? That's easier said than done, something as simple as "Crappy weather today" instead of "I saw a glimpse of the sun." It's just where my mind would go.

I had no trouble in the world of counseling psychology, because you explore with clients in a nonjudgmental way. That's easier when the person is high-functioning. It's just when the cognitive part of the cognitive behavioral doesn't work, you have to go to another form. I found myself doing that – *What's the best that can happen? What's the worst that can happen?* I didn't use those words but that's what I was doing. I wasn't going to die if somebody criticized me. But not having opinions is a childhood thing that has continued.

I've struggled so much with intuition because with engineering in general there's no gray. I come from the place of all objective reasoning, no subjective reasoning. It either is or it isn't. I started consulting with a company in Switzerland in 1993, and it was the first time I was being asked to give an answer on the spot, which is so contradictory to my training as an academic professor, someone who doesn't give an answer about something until I've got all my ducks in a row. In the world of consulting, they talk about "shooting from the hip," whereas I was trained in high-level, academic universities where that's violating the code. My clients wanted a shoot-from-the-hip answer. And that started breaking me out of the rigidity of total objective reasoning.

I got out of my comfort zone, which is really tough to do unless I know the opinion to be correct. I had angst with a capital A, because *What are they going to do with me if I give the wrong answer*? It turns out sometimes they don't care whether you've given the right answer or not. All they need is an answer, because they're responsible to their manager, who they're about to report to that "Our consultant said this." Those first couple of years were very, very tough.

There's a link between starting consulting in 1993 and that next step in evolution in 1996 where I wasn't going to be held hostage for personal-related things. First I experimented in essentially a business environment; then started experimenting with myself. It was also about that time that I began to be disenchanted with academia, because I'd been there, done that, and was ready to be more challenged. Not many people leave the world of academia, because it's a guaranteed-for-life position and income, yet I didn't have any problem walking away after 25 years.

I'd become a full professor, had a very well-established international textbook, and didn't care whether I was in trouble or not with the university, so that's when I started doing the industrial consulting during the summers and for one month in the winter. Most professors don't do that. That was the beginning of the end of academia. The time scale in academia was way too long. And perhaps this links to the consulting and the quick answers. I was moving from time scales on the order of years to time scales on the order of weeks and months. And I continued to move in that direction in my now career back in industry, which is fast-paced. It's just that being a consummate Nine, it sometimes has taken me forever to make a decision. I spent the next nine years preparing to leave. But I never looked back or had buyer's remorse or regret.

In the mid-nineties I got back into martial arts – I'd been there in the early years of my life – and doing a lot of sparring. One of the facets of it was kick boxing. This was a more severe, kind of eclectic martial arts. I was very afraid of kick boxing, but I made myself do it, continued to go and spar until I got good at it, and then I quit. When I was not practicing before I went back, I was vicariously in the martial arts through movies. So whether doing it vicariously or in the moment I've been drawn to martial arts. It isn't about kicking somebody's ass, or about the good guy winning, it's more about the form and control, and the beauty. Otherwise I can't tell you the number of times I've been walked over with perfect volunteer posture.

One of the ways I've changed, which came out of the training in counseling psychology, is in listening without giving advice. Just listening, where I don't feel I have to put my two cents in under some mistaken impression that someone will get the warm fuzzies about me. Typically, academicians can't keep quiet. A friend drives me crazy sometimes because he can't just listen without bringing in his story. It's like a story one-upmanship. I can be guilty of that also, and I'm getting better at listening and not having the need to show what I know. I think I do a good job of it. I've had to in order to reconnect with my oldest daughter. We've had a rocky relationship over the decades and I had to become a listener because I was the only one she could turn to, from an intimate perspective, to talk safely without me giving her advice. And that doesn't mean I didn't want to give advice, but I'm very cognizant of just listening, and in a large number of circles. I was at a dinner party a couple of weeks ago and I was very good at listening. And it isn't withdrawing. It's active listening, so I'm present and not doing what I used to do, which is shut down and drop out.

In earlier years, if I wanted to shut my daughter down, I'd start being a know-it-all, which is basically a mask for insecurity. Trust and intimacy are very connected. I have created a stronger intimacy with my daughter by her having built trust in me. We built the trust because I'm not about to admonish her, correct, or redirect, or give advice unless she asks for it.

Sometimes it's damned hard! I can do it by using active listening and especially looking at body language. Maybe it's intuition, but I can tell where I've crossed the line almost every time, when the other person seems interested, and all of a sudden disconnects. Not always, but in general, that's it. I have my slips, but with my daughter I have a fairly good track record for some years now.

I observe in myself on a number of fronts that I can be in a reverted state when I'm not mentally, spiritually, emotionally grounded. I get myself in trouble by not taking time out for myself – a personal vacation, retreat, or meditative practice. When I take some *me* time, time out for myself or even being with others, I reground myself and then I get back on track. For example, in a work situation before Christmas, if I had been more mentally, emotionally, spiritually grounded, or some combination of those, I wouldn't have let myself talk back to this guy who's one or two levels above me in the management hierarchy. So part of what I'd call passive-aggressive behavior, as an example, will never come when I'm mentally and emotionally rested and spiritually grounded. Also, I can use continual activity in an avoidance sort of way. If I just keep going and going and going, I don't have to examine *me*. Then comes awareness of what I've done wrong, and then I start being judgmental about myself and critical. I can get in a time scale that may involve weeks or even months of just bat-out-of-hell moving forward in my work, imagining others value it. That's not true. But it helps me avoid myself.

To me the change process is a jagged edge that goes up and comes down, as if you put a bunch of W's upside down, side by side – up-down, up-down shapes. It's a visual to me of two steps forward and one step back, going up and then sliding down and then going up again.

In the early to mid-nineties, when I got back into martial arts, the kung fu form was fast moving, with weapons as well as the body, and we were required to learn Tai Chi because they wanted us to have the self-discipline of slowness, a yin/yang balance. There were people next door to the Tai Chi classes doing ballroom dancing, which had some structural similarities to what appealed to me about Tai Chi; it wasn't the Fred Astaire/Ginger Rogers American style, where they go frouing around; it was the international ballroom dancing where everything is done with posture and legislated movements.

I've listened to psychologist Wayne Dyer on tape a number of times, and in person a couple of times, and I think he epitomizes that integration, in a push-pull sort of way. Even some forms of yoga to me are very similar – it's all about the balance between beauty and control, form and structure. This is probably why, when I see art, it doesn't matter whether it's modern art, or portrait, or landscape, I see in it lines and form and links to a peaceful integration of elements. Even before we might have known the yin/yang concept existed in our Western upbringing, it's like we knew it before we knew how to label it. It's no wonder it's withstood the millennia. Maybe I'm longing for that same integration.

Commentary

The overused gift of Style Nine is to be peaceful. It's their Ego's way of attracting what the Taoists might call the attention of no attention. And theirs is a great gift: who can be really peaceful is really somebody! The two stories in this chapter illustrate what can happen when people move beyond the story their Egos are telling. When they transform the need to be peaceful into something much more.

In these stories, transformation is experienced as a shifting. For Claire that takes the form of "aligning myself more with an underlying theme that feels most genuine in my life." For Ralph this shift takes the form of being able to ask for what he wants. Each time one of these moments occurs, they shift from somebody to nobody. They illustrate how these moments help to relax Ego's control, so more of their innate selves can emerge.

A common trait of people of Style Nine is indolence, to avoid making decisions that could endanger the Ego's story of striving to be peaceful. Claire describes using the idea of inertia from physics, "you're going somewhere but without taking any actions to change your direction or velocity." It is the shifting that kicks her out of this inertia.

In such moments, when the Ego relaxes, a person of Style Nine can experience the virtue of *Action*, which Jerry Wagner describes as flowing "naturally from the lens of love. When we experience that we are loved and capable of loving, we naturally and spontaneously say 'thank you' and wish to do something in return."

Ralph describes his Ego defense of moving into a withdrawn state when he receives signals from his conversation partner that don't feel comfortable. He charts the profound moments that helped to weaken this withdrawal, moments where he remains present to the other person. This story provides clear examples of how, when Ego is relaxed, a person of Style Nine can experience the higher quality of *Love*, which Jerry Wagner describes as "attention that is freely and gladly given." For Ralph this takes the form of being present to people and "listening without giving advice. Just listening, where I don't feel I have to put my two cents in under some mistaken impression that someone will get the warm fuzzies about me."

The more Ralph stays present, the more he experiences change as two steps forward and one step back. It's like going up and sliding down again and then going up again. It's about a balance between beauty and control, form and structure.

Today, these two people describe in very similar ways how they move beyond the story their Ego is telling. Ralph describes it as listening in a nonjudgmental way, listening without giving advice. Claire asks how she can be present with herself in a supportive way, even when things are difficult. She now views feelings of discomfort as signals to follow, to see what they have to teach her. She visualizes it thus: "Now I'm making that schematic framing of my different roles in life more playful, more positive, more three-dimensional, more enlivening, visualizing boxes and spheres moving through time."

Three questions to ponder:

- How do I withdraw from others when I am together with them?

- When did I last listen without experiencing the impulse to give advice?

- What decision do I need to take in my life and what do I **really** help me take it?

Chapter Ten – Afterword

Mary and CJ, you're both Nines, you've known each other for years. What stimulated your decision to write this book?

Mary: My interest in writing about the process of transformation grew from my own pain, wishing I had models to show the way, and realizing many of us don't know what we're getting into when we commit to greater self-awareness. Shortly after an intensive Naranjo workshop I became clinically depressed and looked for insights in Enneagram literature, but the only resources at the time were theoretical. Luckily I found a Jungian psychologist who knew the Enneagram and helped me see my depression as a *dark night of the soul*. He paralleled Jungian individuation with the process of spiritual discernment, how we feel consoled as things come together and disconsolate when we struggle. Suddenly I had not only the mournful *this hurts* view, but also *wouldn't it be wonderful if people could read, from an Enneagram perspective, real-life stories of the joys and struggles of awakening*? It became a calling for me, and a gift, because the people who appear in these pages were so inspiring as they described their journeys.

CJ: There are two connected reasons why I was drawn to co-authoring this book. First, in most Enneagram publications the author's point of view seems to be on a different level than the reader's. I'm much more interested in what real people talk about, what they do in their development, what they do in their waking up. Second, I had an idea for a similar book many years ago, something along the lines of *Portraits in Growth* or *Portraits in Transformation*, where I'd collect photographs of places that have special meaning to people and, on a companion page, they'd describe what this place means to them and what helps them with their development.

You've asked others how they define transformation. What is your definition?

CJ: To be honest, I try to avoid labeling the process of change. I've had so many different experiences with my clients, watching how people wake up to themselves, wake up to possibilities. For me it's not just a question of someone reaching a stage of development in their life, it's got to do with *How does that play out?* while at the same time remembering we're still human. Or, as Anthony de Mello put it, "Before I became enlightened I used to get depressed. Since enlightenment I still get depressed."

I don't know if it's marketing, but some people sell seminars, courses or retreats to help people see more clearly, and their material often suggests that suddenly, if you do all this; life's going to be perfect as in picture-book perfect. Life is fine as it is. It's not picture-book perfect like Hallmark or Disney. So the thing is to see things as they are and respond in the appropriate way – and what's appropriate is going to come out of that moment. If I'm in an interaction and I can see clearly what's happening, how do I respond?

I once heard someone share his story that included his wife's suicide. She had attempted it many times before, which the rest of us didn't know, and he said on this particular evening he decided she clearly didn't want to stay alive on this planet anymore, so for him it was no longer a question of what's right or what's wrong. He asked, *What's the loving thing to do?* And when she decided to walk out into the freezing ocean he didn't stop her. This was the person he loved most on this planet. I use his question a lot.

What comes to me is *discernment*, because what's right or wrong is not black and white. And when it's possible to bring that to a coaching or workshop setting, it can support really great things for clients. So often I start out with no fixed idea of what the working process is going to be. I might say "Well, I have an idea of what the next half hour might look like, but maybe we could go a different direction here." And something else opens up. I say this with humility – I know there *will* be an answer. There will be a next step we can take together to help them figure out what they need to understand, or do, or accept.

Mary: For me, a transforming moment is either a bolt of lightning or a minor electric shock. In either case, we suddenly *get* something about ourselves. Not, *I was this kind of person and now I'm a better kind of person*, but rather remembering essence, seeing past ego. In Enneagram terms, transforming has to do with discovering how our Enneagram styles have been a habitual, mechanistic response, and coming to freer choices. The change is from being asleep, in a trance, to awakening.

There's a story about a man working for Gurdjieff who really irritated people, would just set their teeth on edge, and they'd play tricks on the man. Finally, they did something so nasty the guy said, "I've had it, I'm going to leave!" And Gurdjieff said, "You can't leave. I'll pay you twice what I was paying you before," because he realized the irritation this man brought to the group was helping them understand themselves. When we start being mindful, we see parts of ourselves we've never seen before. We're different without ever saying, *I'm going to be different.*

Describe your own transformational experiences:

Mary: I've done a lot of work on myself, but I was thirty years old the first time I became the least bit self-aware. I went to a weekend t-group because my first husband and our best friends had been in one, and I didn't know what a T-group was. My first day there someone pointed out that I seemed angry. I thought, *Who, me? I've never been angry in my life!* They helped me express the anger, and after that weekend I had dreams of hitting my husband over the head with a frying pan. I didn't learn about the Enneagram for another 20 years, but in retrospect that was the first insight into my Nine trance.

Always, the precursor to change in me has been a deep discomfort, depression, dissatisfaction, or anxiety, feeling discombobulated, confused – wondering *What is going on here?* These states move me to do a search, which might be in part due to my fixation of seeking structure, but if I stay open in that process, I learn something about myself, something happens that's beyond my efforts. I had anxiety attacks when I had to stand in front of the room in graduate school, so I took assertiveness training. In an incremental way I was changed, in that I was able to get past the anxiety. It was an attitudinal shift, not truly transformational, but part of my evolution, the beginning awareness.

And I've done a huge amount of reading. My doctoral dissertation was an example of that. I learned so much about my own authority issues as I examined the dynamics of hierarchy and authority relationships that I wrote in the foreword, *I don't know if I wrote the dissertation or the dissertation wrote me.*

My self-awareness has been much more intensified since I learned the Enneagram. A few months after a Naranjo workshop, for example, my cat became very ill. I felt tremendous guilt because I'd been on a twelve-day trip and left him alone except for someone coming in once a day to feed him. By the time I returned he'd lost three pounds, wouldn't eat, and I became obsessed with making him well. My ego was in control. I completely merged with the cat for almost two weeks. Then one morning I fell to my knees. *I can't do this anymore! I can't make this happen!* I looked at him and from the deepest part of my heart said, "I love you and I don't want you to die, but you have to decide, and I will accept it either way." And from that moment the cat started to get better. The shift was in seeing how my obsession to control things, my resistance to taking a deep breath and being with the process, kept me from letting my cat heal. I was trying to *make* it happen, stuffing food down his throat so much he couldn't possibly take over himself. And that's a good analogy for what we all do. Ego's need to be in control is the very thing that keeps us from being present.

My depression had started in 1998 when I was also burning out from coaching corporate clients, thinking *I want to take them deeper, but I don't know how.* I came to see I'd been trying to force my clients' change in the same way I'd force-fed my cat. Until I went through the pain of seeing my Ego's controlling nature, I couldn't take other people to that point.

I've also engaged in what Naranjo calls The Holy War, where there's a tangible *battle* with Ego. Once my second husband and I stopped at a hotel on our way to a boat show. As we were unpacking in our room around 5:30 I said I'd like to do some yoga before dinner and he said, "I'll go to the sauna with my book while you do your yoga, and then we'll go to dinner." An Enneagram Eight, he loves excess, loves to get *really* hot, and I knew – nyaa, nyaa, nyaa – he would fall asleep in the sauna and be late. Of course he was late, and the anger I felt was really heavy. I was quietly processing through dinner, and when we got back to the room he fell asleep immediately but I couldn't sleep. Wondering *What do I do?* I sat in a chair and felt as if I were involved in an exorcism. The anger couldn't have been more real if I'd had to physically wrestle with it. I wasn't trying to wrestle it down, just trying to stay centered and not let it wrestle me down. This went on for what may have been minutes but seemed a lifetime. Then, suddenly, the anger let go, as if my ego understood, *Oh, she really means it. The game is over for this round.* But I was perspiring, felt like I was coming out of a boxing ring, and was physically exhausted the next day.

CJ: My way of coming into all of this was growing up in an alcoholic home. By the time I got to my mid-twenties my life didn't look very good, so I started going to Al-Anon meetings and was introduced to the Twelve Steps. That helped me start seeing life a lot differently and also to begin behaving differently – best summed up in Mello's words: *Perceive clearly and respond accurately*. That's his definition of love. So the waking up part is perceiving clearly, dropping the things that get in the way. In Enneagram terms we're talking about ego fixations. How can we turn down the volume on those? And once we've done that and hear it a bit more like it is, how do we respond?

One major shift was in my *S-Index*, which was how I counted how many shit days I was having every month. My *S-Index* when I started Al-Anon was about 28 or 29. I decided it was time for a change. After a couple of years in Al-Anon, going to meetings four or five times a week and having long conversations into the evenings, my *S-Index* dropped dramatically down to 1 or 2. So that period from age 25 to 29 was quite intense from a developing perspective, and most of it was just doing the Twelve Steps. I was written off by most of the doctors while a baby and I'm still here, so when life was quite rocky many years later, those qualities were what helped me to keep going.

With the *S-Index* there was a lot of unacknowledged anger. I can remember a couple of years into Al-Anon the theme of the meeting was anger and I said, "I'm the only person in the room who doesn't get angry." When I could see that a bit more clearly, about a year later, I thought, *Whoops!* and realized the anger had been seeping out of me all those years, in the form of sarcasm, for example. Life was quite complicated in a family with an active alcoholic, not knowing from one day to the next, or even from one hour to the next, what life was going to be like in any shape or form. That also makes trust a big issue, because the only thing that was clear about a promise was that it wouldn't be kept. Not out of badness, but my mother's relationship with the bottle was stronger than her relationship with the people around. Fortunately that's changed: she got into recovery before I got into Al-Anon. I began to focus on developing gratitude and learning about the importance of letting go, which is a continual and ongoing process. There's always something else to let go of.

Later, there were a couple of very important experiences. Fast-forwarding into my late thirties when I came into the particular line of work I'm in now. I'd risen in the organization and was a program director for research in ABB, a large, multinational Swiss/Swedish equivalent of G.E., managing about eighty people worldwide. It was a fun job and they were thinking about preparing me for a step up. I could have ended up running one of the business units or maybe gone farther; who knows? I said "I'd better think about it." That summer of 1998 I was in a ten-day program called *Nature as the Source of Power*. I'd been on a long walk reflecting back on my life, stopped for a rest, had this moment of clarity looking out at the Alps, knew what I was supposed to be doing, and *It's not what I'm doing now*. I identified the ingredients for what I was supposed to be doing but misread them at first, coming up with a career that didn't work out, which was OK. I made the decision to quit my job, not knowing what was going to come next.

As you can imagine, the reaction of my parents, my siblings, my partner, my friends was, "Are you nuts?" I said "I don't think so, but something has to change." I was enjoying the job I was doing but had this knowing, *It's not what I'm supposed to be doing in life*. The job was very seductive because it was fun and well-paid, lots of interesting people to meet; *what's not to like about the whole thing?* Yet I knew it wasn't right for me. I came back from that vacation, made sure I got all my people's research funded for the next year, and as soon as that conversation was finished said to my boss, "There's one more thing we have to talk about today." He said "What's that?" And I said "I quit." He was an Eight, so he liked it simple. His response was "Tell me more." I explained it to him and he said "That's great! How can I help?" That was a big change and a big waking up, getting out of the comfort zone. Being too comfortable is a danger, not just for Nines, of falling asleep.

The next important experience came in 2001 over the space of about six weeks. I first did a family constellation and what emerged was the place of my older, dead brother in the family. Because when I was born, I wasn't supposed to live very long, and the nurse said, "Quick, I need a name," my mother blurted out the name of my brother who'd died. So I had *his* name. That's when I made the shift from Conor to CJ, to leave the name for him because he had it first. Then two weeks later my wife came home and said, "I've met somebody else." So identity had just disappeared, a relationship had just disappeared, and four weeks after that – the night before I was going back to Switzerland to sign a contract guaranteed for two years to consult for two days a week – the guy I was contracting with said, "We're not signing." This shift was a huge lesson in detachment. There wasn't much left to be attached to at that point, and at the same time I realized, *With all that gone, I'm still OK.* To go back to our good friend Tai Chi, which I'd been practicing since 1987: *the punch of no-punch, the structure of no structure.* That was when I started to deepen my Enneagram work, went to the professional EPTP near Heidelberg.

Two more transforming experiences I'll mention briefly. One was in the winter of 2001, a week with a form of bonding theory developed by Dan Casriel, connected with the Enneagram – pretty intense physical work, with holotropic breathing. I went thinking I'd be working on my pending divorce, but what came out of it was working on everything that happened to me during my first eight weeks of life in the intensive care unit. Things happened I can't articulate, but I have a felt memory. My way of rationalizing it is that at that age infants don't have vocabulary. That turned out to be really important to help free up stuff that was getting in the way. After that I began to explore ways to connect the Enneagram and the Twelve Steps.

Then there was the experience at the beginning of 2011, my father's final bout with cancer. On the Thursday evening, my sister called and said, "How soon can you get here?" I got the next plane and was with him all my waking hours during his final few days, helping take care of him. That was a pretty special time, being in the presence of his dignity, thoughtfulness and humour.

What has changed for you? How are you different?

CJ: David Daniels said once, "When we notice we're in our trance, we have a choice whether we want to do something else or whether we want to stay in there." I've become much more in touch with observing myself, releasing, detaching from things, learning to appreciate and savor and notice more. The Casriel work helped me get physically in touch with my feelings. To really experience feelings and what's getting in the way brings another dimension of joy to life. It doesn't mean I can do it all the time.

I've had people say I'm not a Nine, I can't be a Nine because of the poetry and songs I've written. One person said, "You can't be a Nine because you've edited Liz's book *and* the Journal this year." There's a danger of all this turning into some sort of competitive context. I've heard people use the Levels of Development with comments to me like, "Oh, you're only Level 3." There's a way the person says that where clearly they're at some higher level of the universe and deign to talk to a low-life for a few minutes. Attachment to Level can be dangerous. We Nines get stuff done. However, we sometimes get stuff done at the price of forgetting ourselves. So it's keeping that balance.

Mary: My whole perception has changed. It's boiled down to something very simple, that the *only* work is noticing how your patterns operate. Everything else is camouflage. Religious traditions say this in some form: *Center yourself and open yourself to real connection with Spirit, and here's how to keep the habits of the mind from interfering.* At least 20 minutes a day I practice Qigong and/or mantra meditation, knowing if I do this, Ego is out of luck. Even *trying not to* let monkey mind take over is ego-driven. The place to be is not where I DON'T WANT to be, but where I AM. I think mindfulness is the only way to deal with attachments.

In a workshop someone asked Claudio Naranjo, "How are people different as they become transformed?" and he said, "On the outside they may look very much the same." I think that's true. The difference is in what happens internally when my patterns come up. I sort differently. I experience differently. I'm more open to myself and my foibles. I'm hooked less often and the struggles aren't as difficult. I more readily know what I'm feeling and make conscious choices. I'm much more loving and forgiving of myself. For as long as I live, my stuff may keep showing up, but I'm coming to love myself anyway.

There are some specific ways I'm different. I love to coach – I'm exhilarated by it. I may occasionally be a little nervous, especially with a new client, but not in the way I would have been 20 years ago. I'm much better able to be present and enjoy life as it shows up. I'm more accepting of relationships and far less judgmental. I may not look any different on the outside, but others don't know the judgments I used to carry internally. As I become less self-judging, it very naturally flows outward.

I'm more aware of how distractibility can keep me from my own agenda. This has led to the most important and visible change – finding my voice: having opinions, writing, being an Enneagram coach and mentor. I also tell people who I am without fear of how they'll judge me. The more I write, the freer I become of worrying *What will people think of me?* I'd been brewing the writing since I was in my twenties. I published some articles and a book with mentors in graduate school, but those were not initiated by me and I hadn't come to the point of saying, *I want to be a writer*. Those wishes were underground until a therapist said, "Do you hear yourself?" And I realized, *Oh yes, there I am*!

What resources have helped?

Mary: I'm forthcoming about what's going on with me, and I discover myself as I talk. So if I find myself in a stuck place, I go to a therapist. But I could never be in therapy for years. I need closure: *OK, I've worked on some stuff, I've gotten some tools; now I need to be on my own for a while and try it out*. But every few years I'll go through several months of counseling. Other than that, my primary resources have been friends and books. I have moments with books that are like falling in love. Something comes over me, a kind of knowing: *This is important for you on your path*. It goes beyond intellectual input; it's an emotional engagement with what I'm reading, a moment of blissful awareness that I'm on the right track. Books becomes guides for me; they help me integrate.

Friends have been a terrific resource and I'm selective; I pick really good friends. The year I was to become 50 I made a New Year's resolution to surround myself with spiritual people. Later, when I was so depressed, one such friend said, "Isn't it interesting how your body has given you a depression, forcing you to stop everything and pay attention to what you needed to hear?" And that's absolutely true. The other thing that rang true was his response when I said I was so depressed that nothing mattered. "Ah!" he mused. "That's sort of Zen, isn't it? Nothing matters." I *got* it, the whole point of mindfulness; that at some level life is an illusion, nothing that matters to our egos really matters.

With another friend, I was describing my emotional pain over my failing second marriage, and one of her suggestions was to look at what I might have done to create the situation. I dug in my heels, insisting I wasn't part of the problem, then later that night – and I swear it was a specific point in time, a moment so potent for me it was as if someone picked me up and threw me down in a different place, WHOCK!!! – even though it was horrifying to admit, I knew in every fiber of my being it was true: *Why is the other person always the bad guy? My whole life I've made myself a victim!* To say this awareness "came to me" doesn't convey how this experience was beyond words. It wasn't a gradual awakening, it wasn't an intellectual exercise, it was an explosion.

Reading Carl Jung's *Memories, Dreams, Reflections* was reassuring. He did what I want to do, showed the courage to write about his struggles with his own demons, as if to say *I have to show the way, I can't be attached to what people think of me*. His personal experience was what made his psychology so powerful, a perfect example of the Wounded Healer.

I've often been helped by applying coaching techniques to myself. For example, in one of my workshops I took participants through an exercise on projection, suggesting they think of someone who irritated them, then take that in as a projection – "I'm irritated at the (person's name) in me who does (X)." To myself I thought of the weekend before when I'd been in the passenger seat with a friend in the Rallyburgers drive-through lane for almost 20 minutes, and when we got to the window he drove off without our food, because he was so impatient at having to wait that long. I couldn't see any logic to it because we then had to find someplace else to eat, which took *more* time! I tried this on as projection, and it didn't seem to fit while I was teaching, but the next morning I woke up with a terribly uncomfortable sensation I'd never been conscious of before. I did not want to be in my body. Grousing around, I wondered *What the hell is going on*? All of a sudden I *got* it – for the first time in my Niney life of apparent equanimity, I was feeling almost unbearably impatient! When my friend had been impatient I couldn't identify with it. All I could do was play victim and blame him. When I owned this for myself, I let in awareness of my own impatience.

Gendlin's Focusing technique is a helpful way for me to stay with my feelings. With this approach you exaggerate the feeling and look for a label that fits. Beginning with a *felt sense* that something is going on, you stay with it, try on labels until you say *Ah, yes, that's what it's like*. It might be a word, a phrase, *I feel like I'm being burned at the stake and the flames are licking up*. Then there can be what Gendlin calls a *felt shift*, but the process is valuable even if you don't feel the shift. It's not about getting it right; it's the practice that's important. And the more I've engaged in the practice, the more often I've felt the shift.

I'm lucky my body *requires* some of my practices. I'm very physically reactive and if I don't do yoga I get arthritic. Too much coffee or alcohol or sugar stresses my system and I get acid reflux. If I don't practice Qigong I'm tense and a bit depressed.

For many years I've practiced various ways to tap into my intuition. Dreams are especially helpful when I'm stuck, resolving something I've unable to access consciously. Using active imagination with the characters and metaphors in dreams, or the *I Ching*, or Tarot, free me to learn from my unconscious. A number of experiences have helped me be able to do that. I've taken Silva courses, gone to creativity training, attended body/mind workshops. One of Arnold Mindell's dreambody exercises put me in touch with how the tension in my shoulders had been connected to not asking for what I want, and I subsequently weaned myself from a drug for neck pain I'd been using for seven years.

CJ: The Twelve Steps are helpful for perceiving clearly, the Enneagram is a wonderful help. Joseph Campbell is also very important to me. My brother told me about Campbell in 1989 but I didn't really get him. Then, in the car on our way to a retreat weekend, he played a cassette of a Bill Moyers interview with Campbell, who was talking about the early myths, about this primal energy in all the gods. And as he was talking, suddenly a huge storm blew in from the Atlantic, the entire horizon was filled with sheet lightning, and I thought, *OK, I get this now*. This made it click for me. I've gotten an awful lot from *Hero with a Thousand Faces*, listening to tons of Campbell's talks on audio, and from his lecture series on James Joyce and *Ulysses*. I better understand, looking back, how particular phases of my journey have unfolded. They all follow the structure, so far. And Campbell was the one who put together this structure the myths and stories follow. He was also a Nine.

I've tried many other practices – both to help me and so I can suggest something appropriate for clients who are interested.

I've also been increasing my interest over the last number of years in systemic structural constellations, which have a theoretical foundation in Wittgenstein's philosophy, totally different from Hellinger's family constellations, for example. Hellinger has a *normative* view: "This is the way the world is; I'm telling you what it's like. These are the principles your system follows." The difference with systemic structural constellations is it adopts a *curative view*; the attitude is not to say "This is the way it is," but to say "How might it be if...? Many systems follow these principles; maybe this one is different." I love the openness of this stance and it helps to get great results for people.

I've mainly given influences from schools and approaches, but there are many people who are really important to my development. What they brought to the conversation was the ability to totally listen and be unconditionally accepting and supportive. One was a retired doctor and psychologist I saw every week. It was her calling to do this for free, and she was wonderful. She mostly just listened, but the few sentences she did say gave me something to chew over for the next week. The whole time the clearest message was, *No matter how screwed up it looks, I'm totally OK as I am.* Also the power of the *and*. I started with her the summer of 1988, and was on and off with her for about a year and a half.

What have your resistances been?

Mary: One of my resistances to change has been leaving situations because I didn't like the way the teacher was teaching. For example, I paid for a week-long Jean Houston workshop, but because I was annoyed with how full of herself she seemed and for pushing us into self-revelation without first building trust, I left on the second day. I know others who've had similar reactions to Houston, but that's not the point. I would certainly have learned many things about myself in that week if I hadn't let my resistance stop me. I've done the same with some Enneagram teachers, rationalizing my negative judgments as stemming from superior knowledge of the right way to do things.

My most common block is knowing what practices will help, yet not doing them. When coaching I've had to devise ways to help clients get past their defenses. So I certainly know *how* to get past my own, but my resistance hooks me anyway on a regular basis. I hope maybe 80% of the time I see it, stay with it, and eventually it lets go.

CJ: One of my patterns that can get in the way is becoming comfortable and saying, *Well, things have improved and I'm comfortable with how things are now*. The danger for me when I'm comfortable is to just drift off and forget to do the things that keep me awake or help me to wake up. An example is from time to time not thinking about doing the morning practice. It just doesn't occur to me when I wake up, even though I have done it for the previous 30 days. Or to lose my focus and do something irrelevant. I've found that when my working space gets too chaotic I tidy up because it drags me down if I don't. However, once it gets tidy I start to think about how to rearrange everything, which is maybe not the most important thing in that moment. I accept *That's me being a Nine again* in a recognizable way.

I think the greatest challenge in episodes of awakening has been applying and using this in relationships and partnerships. In particular, for a long time I was conflict avoidant. I believe the American phrase is, "I just didn't want to go there." Whereas with conflict we don't have any choice. It's there, parked in front of the door. So a big learning was not to walk away from something when it started to get difficult, but to stay with it and see, *Well, what is it that's difficult? And what's this got to do with me, with the other person, and how we interact?* An area that still needs work.

What's your model or metaphor for transformation?

CJ: My metaphor for these changes is *emerging from the mist*, which fits the experience of growing up in Dublin, a city that gets its share of mist and fog, a cold seaside city. I can remember walking down the street when there was a heavy mist and suddenly somebody emerged from the mist to me, then disappeared. Then the next one came, and the next. It's not a one-off thing. As I go down the street, it's a series of merging, meeting, then back into the mist again because they're going down the street in the other direction. It's this being able to see them clearly that moment. *Perceive clearly, respond accurately.*

Mary: My understanding of Horney, Jung, and Buddhism all flow together in my notion that we develop awareness of a given aspect of

Ego or set of illusions, habits of attention, then we observe how these patterns play out. And usually the first thing we observe is how annoyed we are at what we're seeing, wishing we no longer had these reactions. Then we observe ourselves letting go of judgment. Sometimes we use techniques or practices, sometimes a shift will occur spontaneously. We then recycle; not the same old things coming up over and over, but rather observing the same old things in a different form or at a different level. I see this as an inward spiral. An infinite spiral pointing inward to the Self.

Where are you in the process?

Mary: As an introverted Nine, my experiences of being more present and engaging with others, knowing what I want and putting my voice out in the world are, I pray, a form of *active engagement*, which is the Nine's path. But all my struggles, all my resistances, of course, are very Nine-like – to have been so unaware of myself until I was in my thirties, the ways my idealized *good girl* image fed my victimhood all those years. I'm much less judgmental toward myself, more and more accepting of myself and others. The recycling is occurring, much in the way I experience learning about the Enneagram. I think, *Oh, I understand that now*, and then I engage more deeply and realize, *I know nothing!* And of course, there's always more to learn.

CJ: There was a guy who went to the same Twelve Step meeting every Thursday, and at the end of the meeting we'd have a cup of tea for a half-hour or so, then when he was going I'd say "See you next week, Mick." And he'd say "I *hope* to see you." This went on for eight or nine months. Then I said to him, "Mick, at the end of every meeting I say 'See you next week' and you say 'I *hope* to see you,' and next meeting we see each other. So what's this 'I *hope* to see you'?" And he said, "Well, I'm a Quaker. It's not up to us if we see each other next week or not. If God wills it, it will happen; if not, we won't. So I *hope* to see you, but it's not my decision." And I've found that bit of philosophy to be helpful in dealing with the ups and downs, surprises and changes. I can have the intention to do something or meet someone, but whether or not that totally works out is not necessarily up to me, because there are so many other elements in this complicated system of life, so many

Chapter Ten

different influences. A friend of mine uses an Arab saying, "Pray to Allah and tie up your camel."

One more thing has to do with emotions. The way we speak about and think about emotions impacts how we experience them. So when you say "I feel sad" or "I feel angry" or whatever it is, there's an identification with the emotion. In the Irish language I'd say, "There is a sadness on me." It's as if I'm wearing a coat of sadness, but I can just as easily take it off; there's no identification. It's on me or around me, but I'm not it. It took me a while to wake up to this realization, that my relationship with emotions was not what I was finding in the books, because most of the books are written by people in the States. It's inherent in the English language, unless we're really careful about how we're using language. People don't walk around saying "I'm experiencing anger." They say "I'm mad as hell." So I have this lack of identification and then also ownership of the feeling, where someone else doesn't *make* me feel anything.

It reminds me of the British TV show "The Prisoner" in the 1960s where a guy was being held prisoner in a village. This will be heretical for those in the community for whom the number is the only game in town, but the whole series was about him trying to escape. He had a number, so whoever was running the whole thing communicated with him through a televised system: "Number Six! Don't do that!" and he would scream back, "I am not a number!, I am a free man.".

About the Authors

CJ Fitzsimons, Ph.D., the founder and CEO of Leadership Sculptor, lives in Germany and works internationally. Clients include leading research institutes in Europe and North America, as well as companies like Airbus, BASF, Bayer and Daimler. He is co-editor and co-author of *Internationales Projektmanagement – internationale Zusammenarbeit in der Praxis*, the first book to apply the Enneagram in project management, and three other books on project management. Introduced to the Enneagram in the 1990s, he has been using it in his leadership development work since 2001. He was vice-president of the International Association in 2012—13.

Leadership Sculptor website: http://www.leadershipsculptor.com
Leadership Sculptor blog: http://www.leadershipsculptor.com/blog

Mary R. Bast, Ph.D. is an Enneagram coach who works with clients worldwide by phone. In addition to her Enneagram-related books, which include *Out of the Box Coaching with the Enneagram* and Out of the Box Self-Coaching Workbook, Mary is a poet (*Eeek Love; Time Warp; Toward the River; Unmuzzled, Unfettered*), memoirist (*Autobiography Passed Through the Sieve of Maya*), artist (www.marybast.com), and editor in chief of *Bacopa Literary Review*. Learn more about Mary's books and blogs on her Amazon.com author page.

Out of the Box Coaching Web Site: http://www.breakoutofthebox.com
Coach Mentor Blog: http://mentoringforcoaches.blogspot.com
Out of the Box Self-Coaching Tips Blog:
http://outoftheboxcoaching.blogspot.com
Mary Bast Fine Art: http://www.marybast.com
Poetry and Found Poetry by Mary Bast: http://windingsheets.blogspot.com

About Leadership Sculptor

Leadership Sculptor GmbH is at the forefront of professional leadership development, providing innovative, tailored training and coaching for performance improvement with leaders in scientific and engineering research.

For more than 18 years, Leadership Sculptor has delivered creative, practical and custom-built development programs to fulfill its mission of challenging habitual ways of thinking, creating value and supporting bottom-line results to customers internationally. Leadership Sculptor is a consultancy headquartered in Baden-Baden, Germany. Leadership Sculptor Press publishes books that help leaders develop their personal and leadership capacities.

For more information on Leadership Sculptor development programs, upcoming events, or publications, contact us at +49 (172) 737 45 09, email info@leadershipsculptor.com or visit us online at www.leadershipsculptor.com.

Download your bonus resource

As a thank you for purchasing this book, download your complimentary copy of the Somebody? Nobody? workbook from http://leadershipsculptor.com/wp-content/uploads/2017/11/Workbook.pdf It contains all the reflection questions in the book and space for your personal reflections.

Get further help for your development and growth

If you have benefited from this and are interested in bringing its message to your organisation, please contact info@leadershipsculptor.com for information about

- a talk on how leaders can use the Enneagram in their personal and leadership development
- coaching for development, growth and the Enneagram
- workshops and presentations on personal and leadership development using the Enneagram.

Made in the USA
Monee, IL
13 September 2020